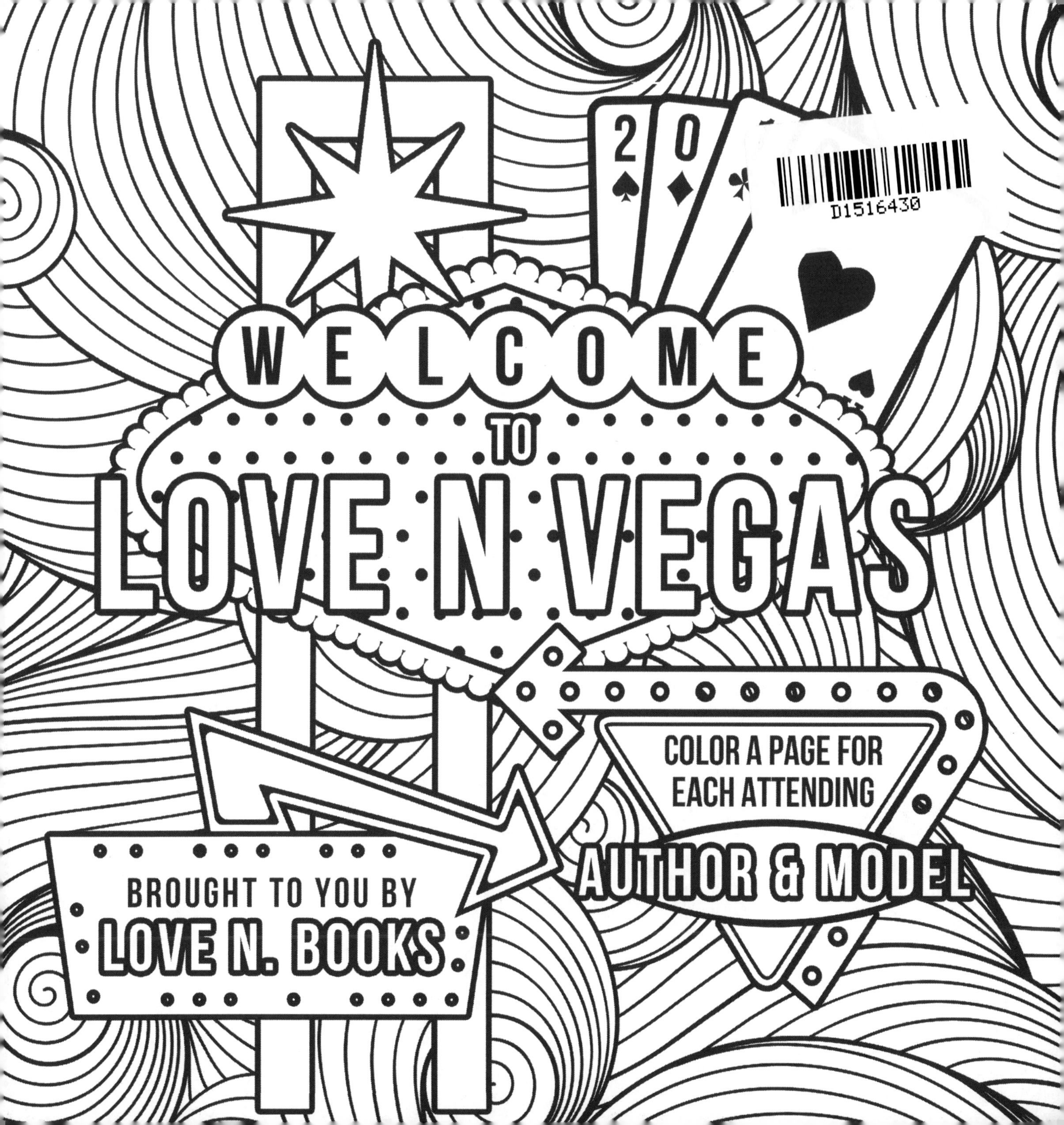
WELCOME
TO
LOVE N VEGAS
COLOR A PAGE FOR
EACH ATTENDING
AUTHOR & MODEL
BROUGHT TO YOU BY
LOVE N. BOOKS

LOVE N. VEGAS 2016

Cover and Pages by: Jessica Hildreth at Creative Book Concepts/Love N. Creations

ISBN-13: 978-1533381057

Printed in U.S.A

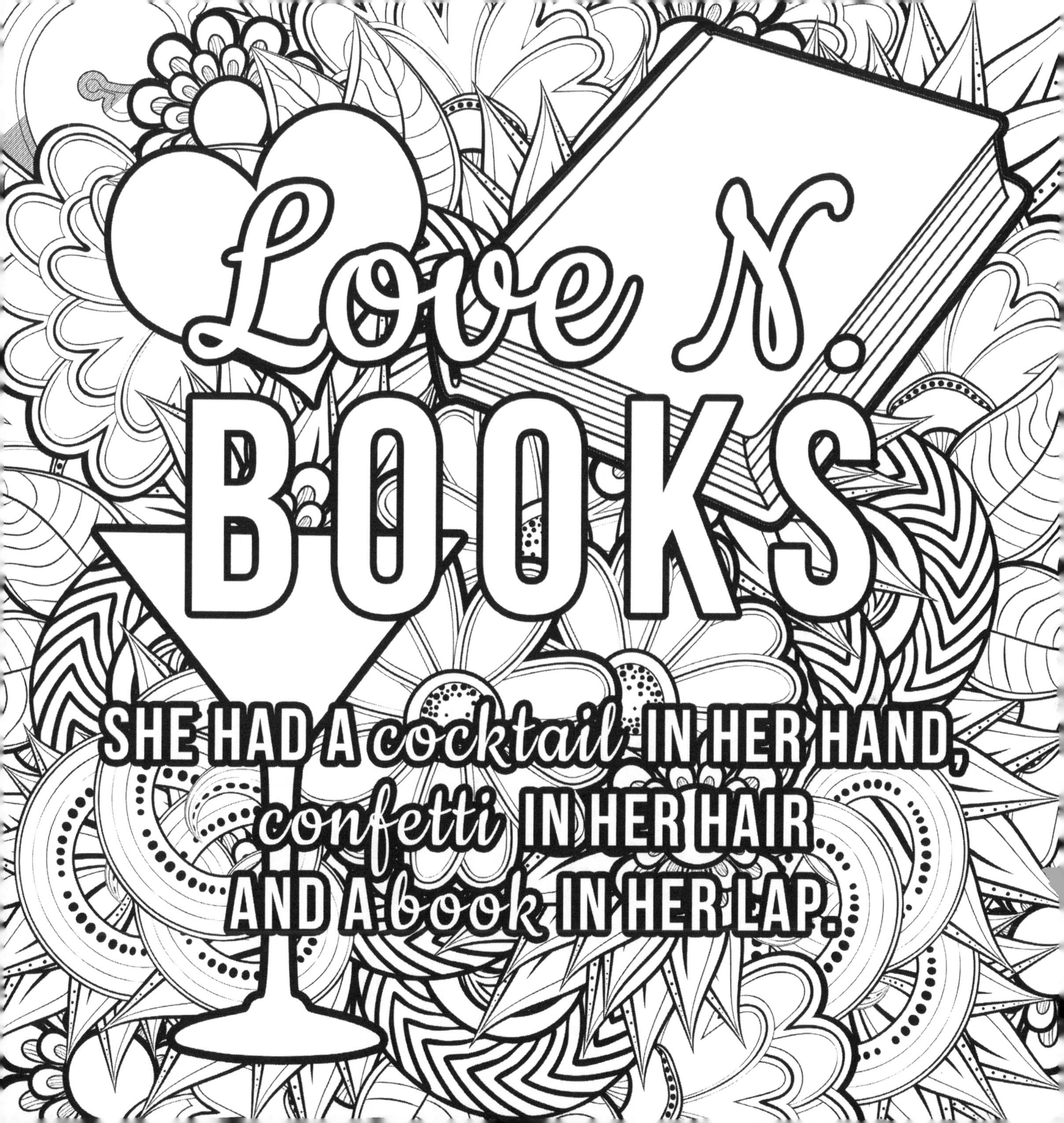
Love N. BOOKS
SHE HAD A cocktail IN HER HAND,
confetti IN HER HAIR
AND A book IN HER LAP.

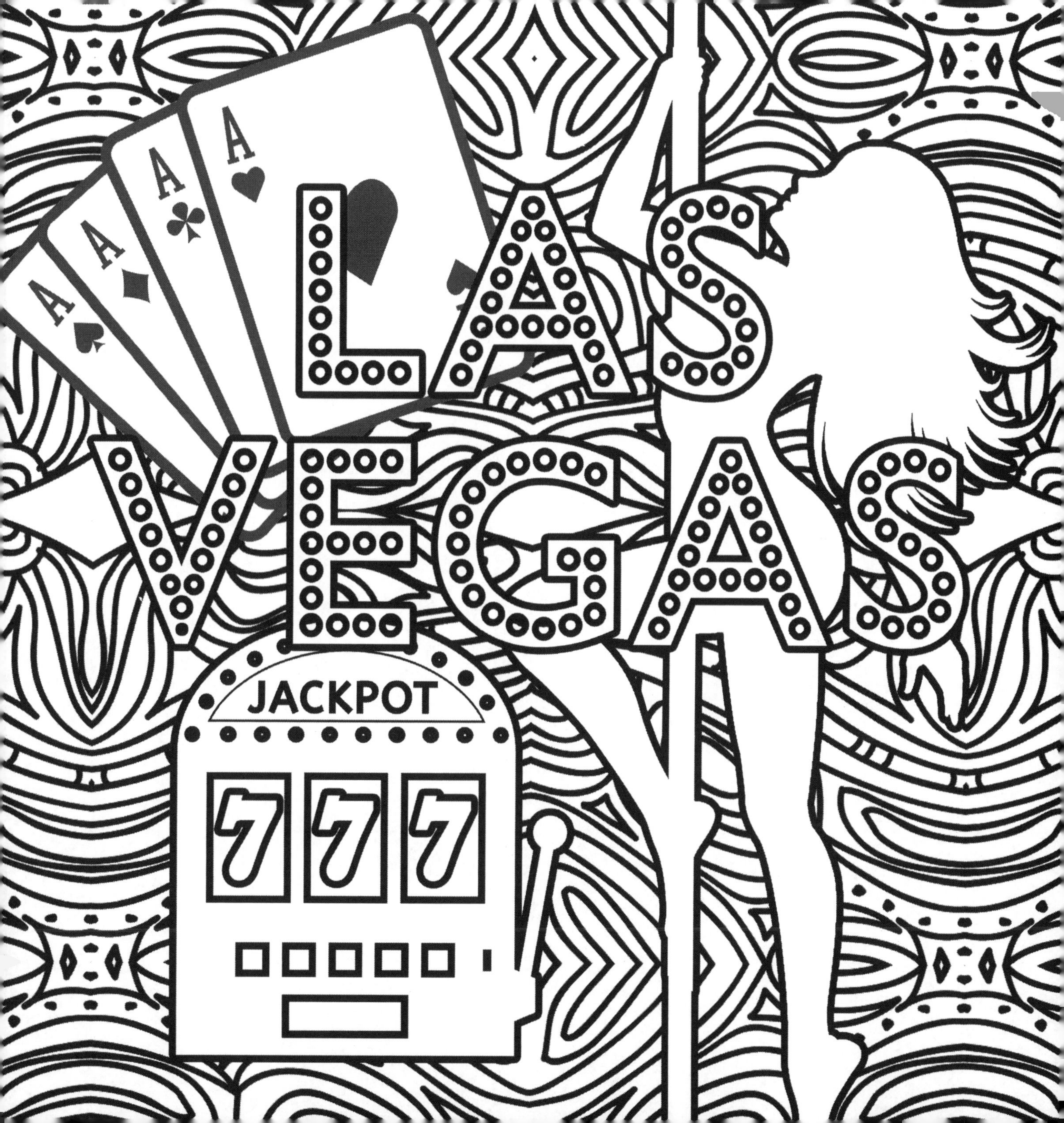
LAS
VEGAS
JACKPOT
777

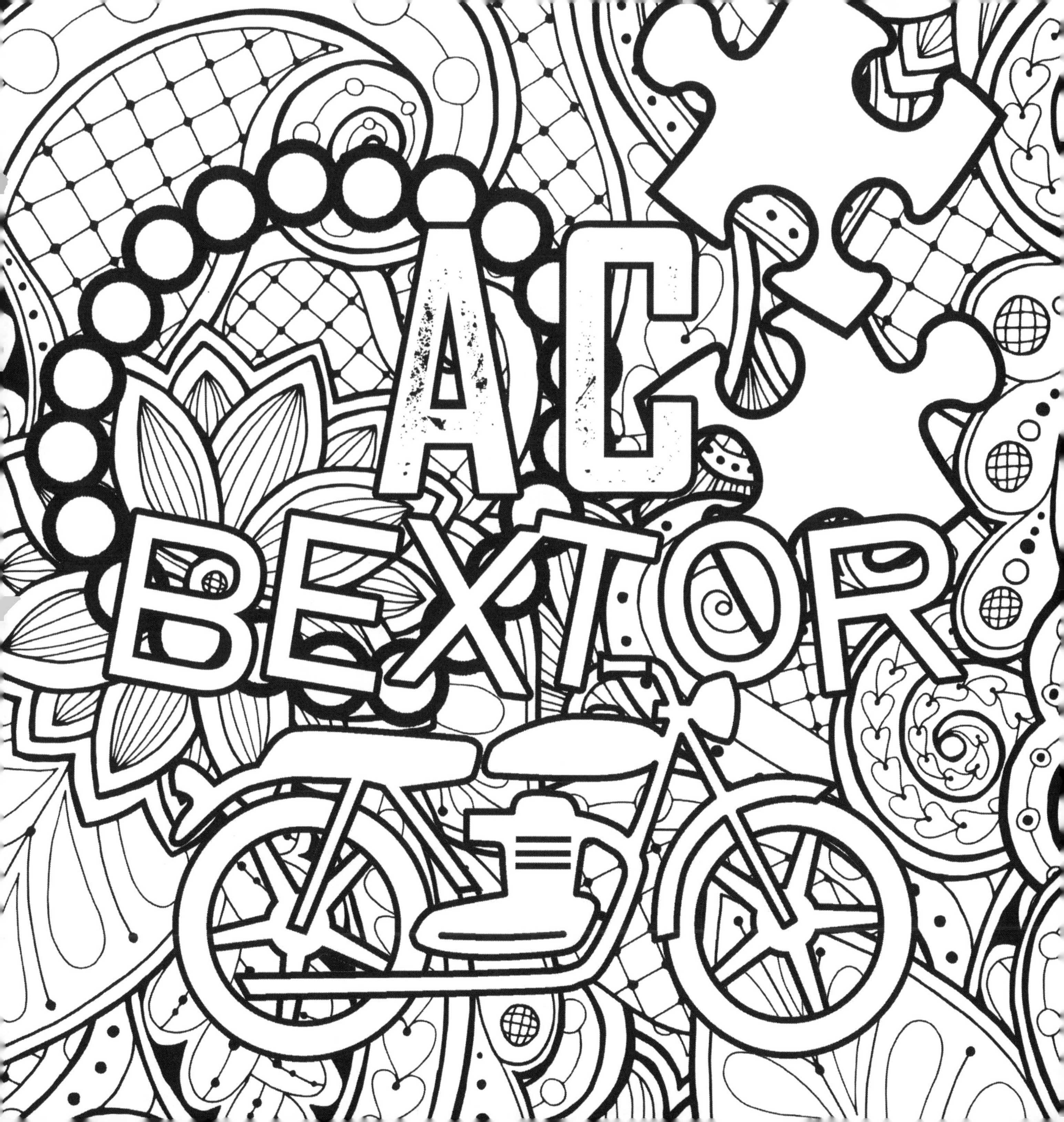
AC
BEXTOR

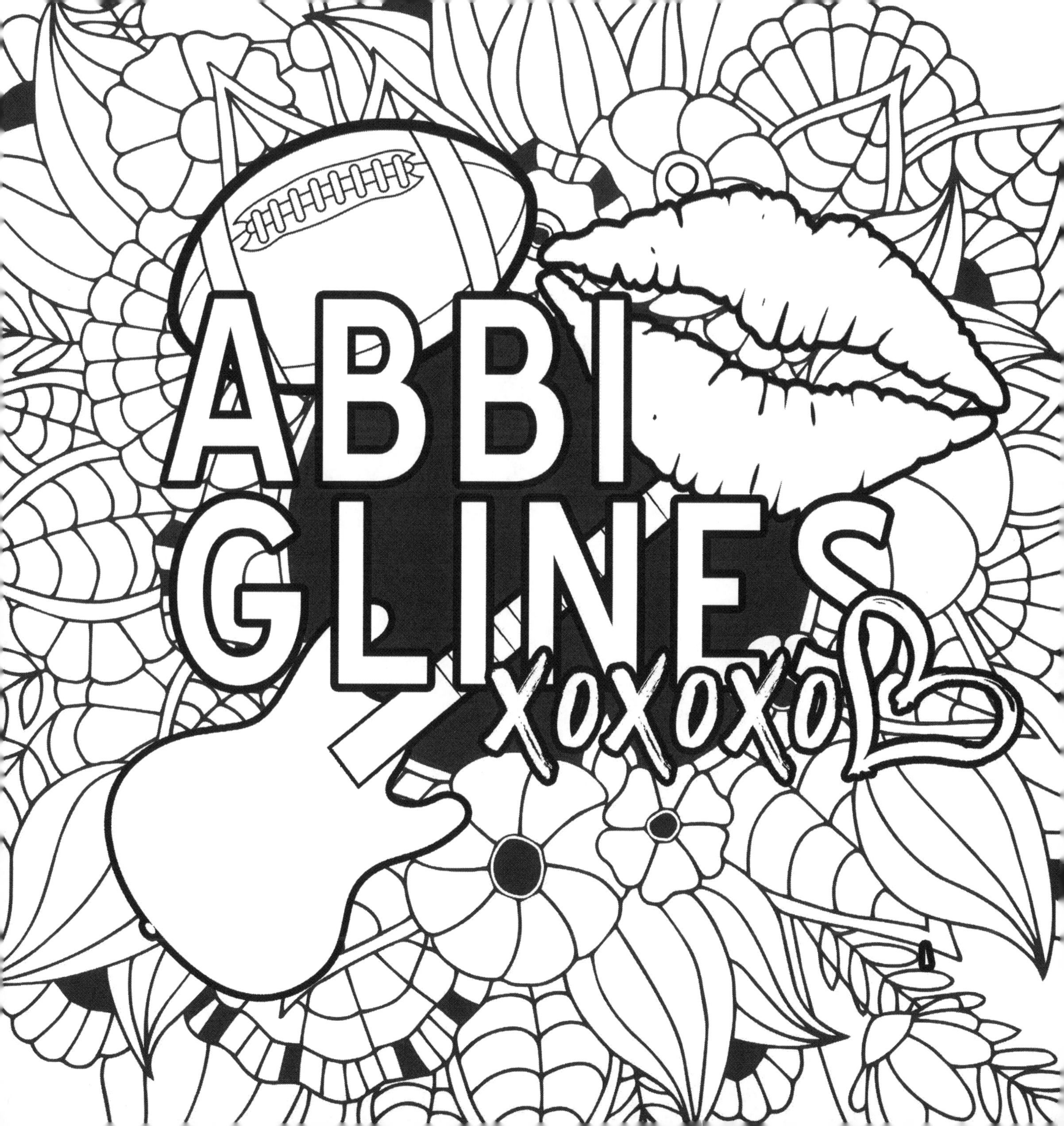
ABBI
GLINES
XOXOXO

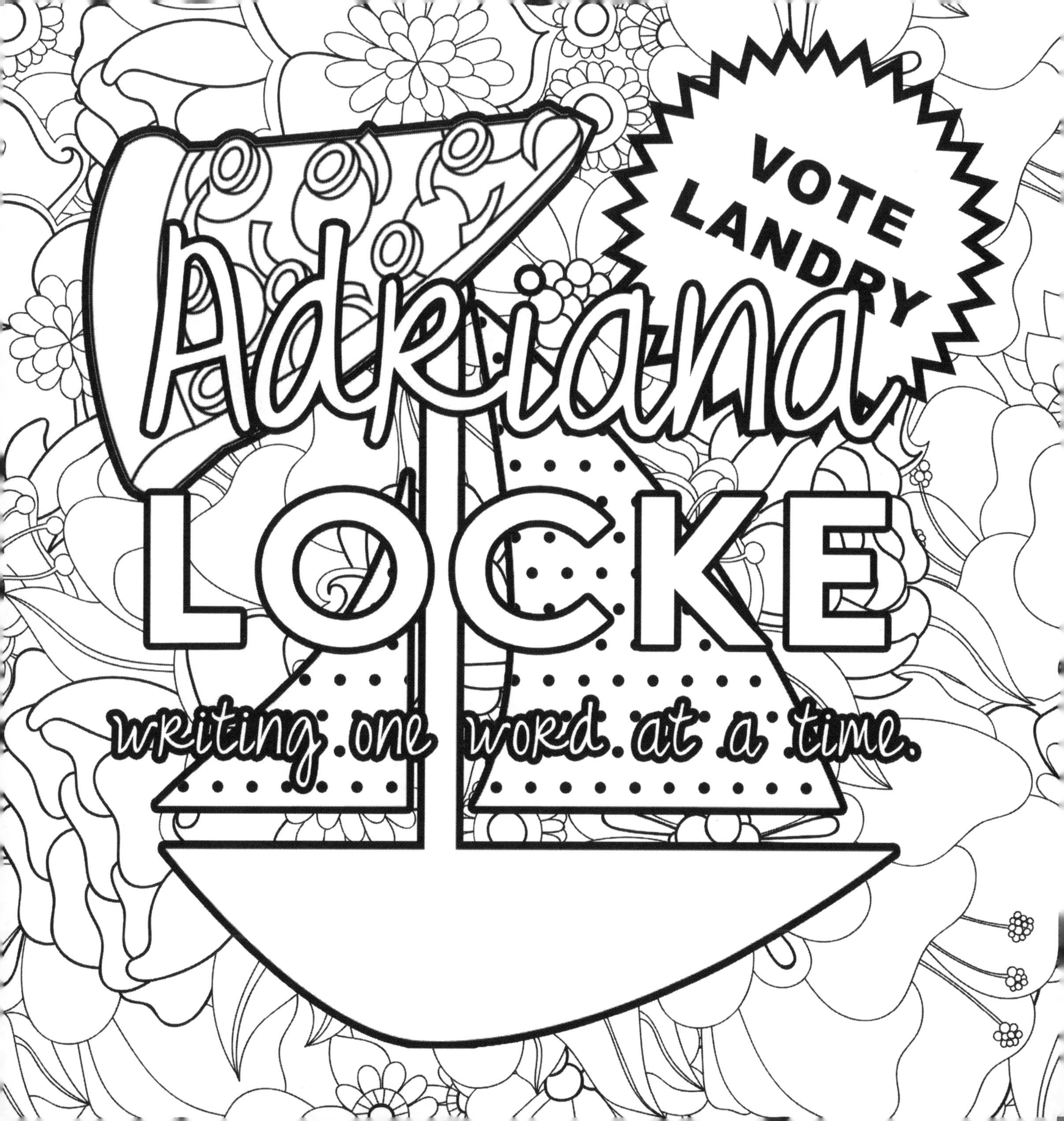
VOTE
LANDRY
Adriana
LOCKE
writing one word at a time.

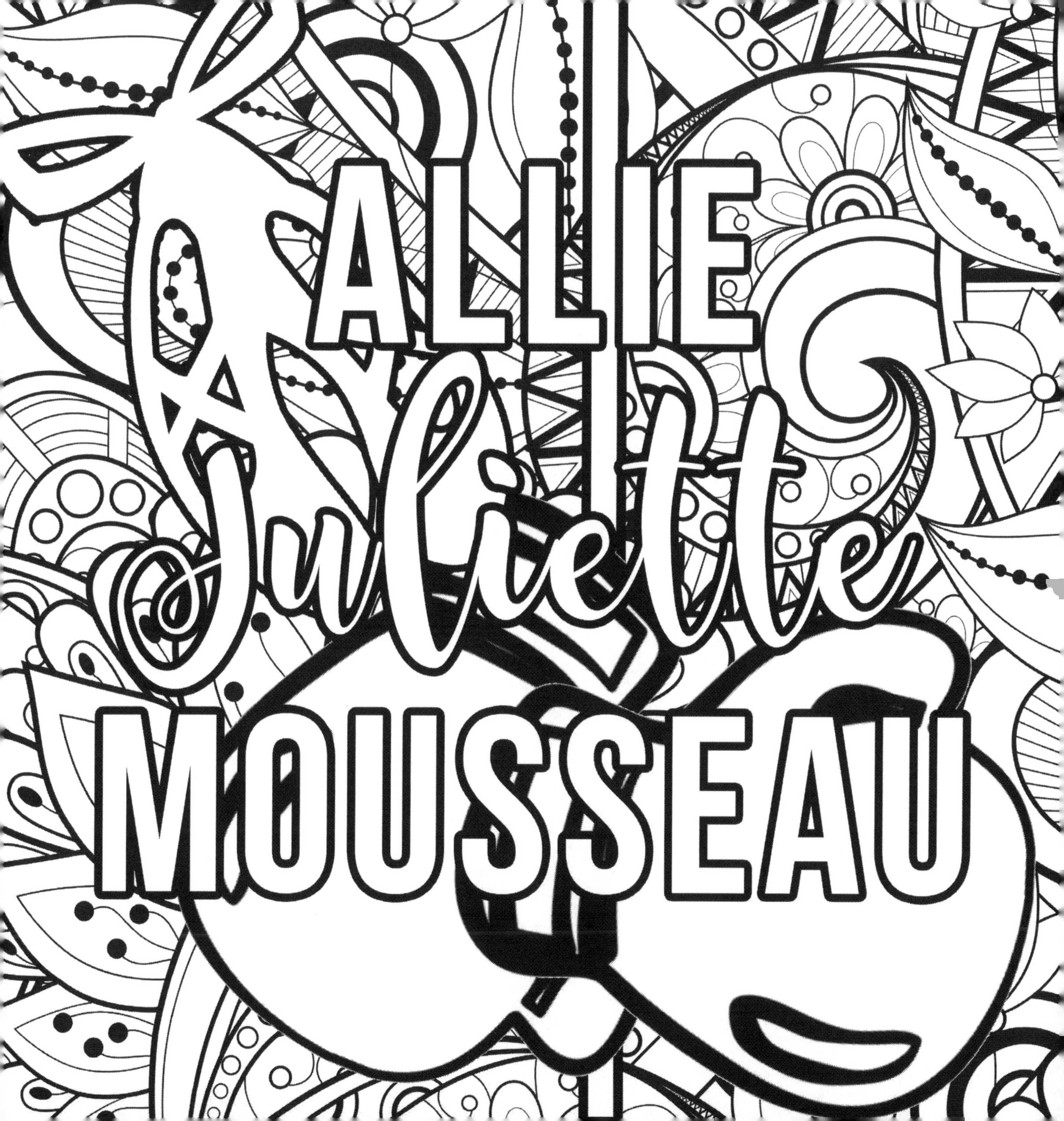
ALLIE
Juliette
MOUSSEAU

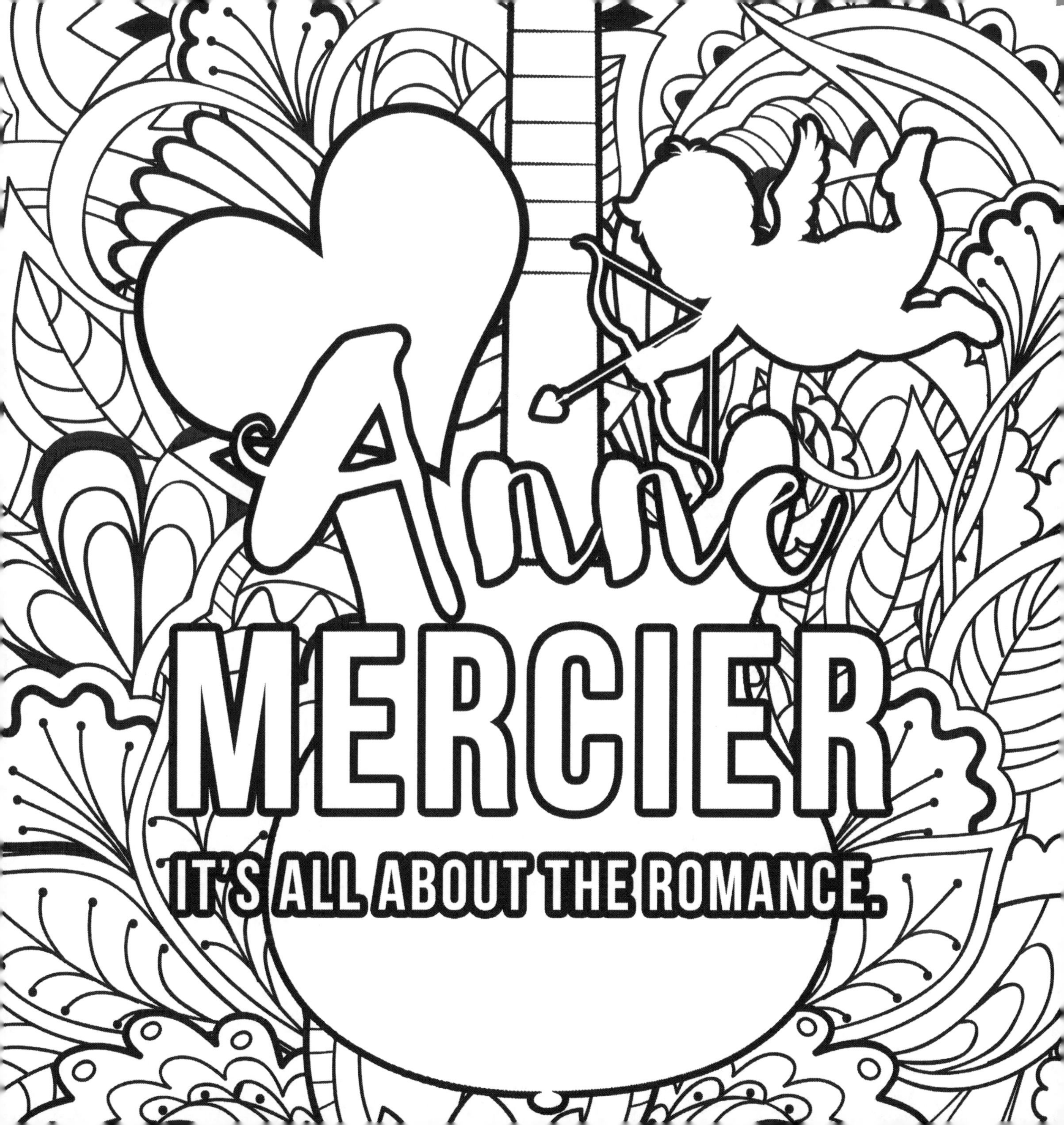
Anne
MERCIER
IT'S ALL ABOUT THE ROMANCE.

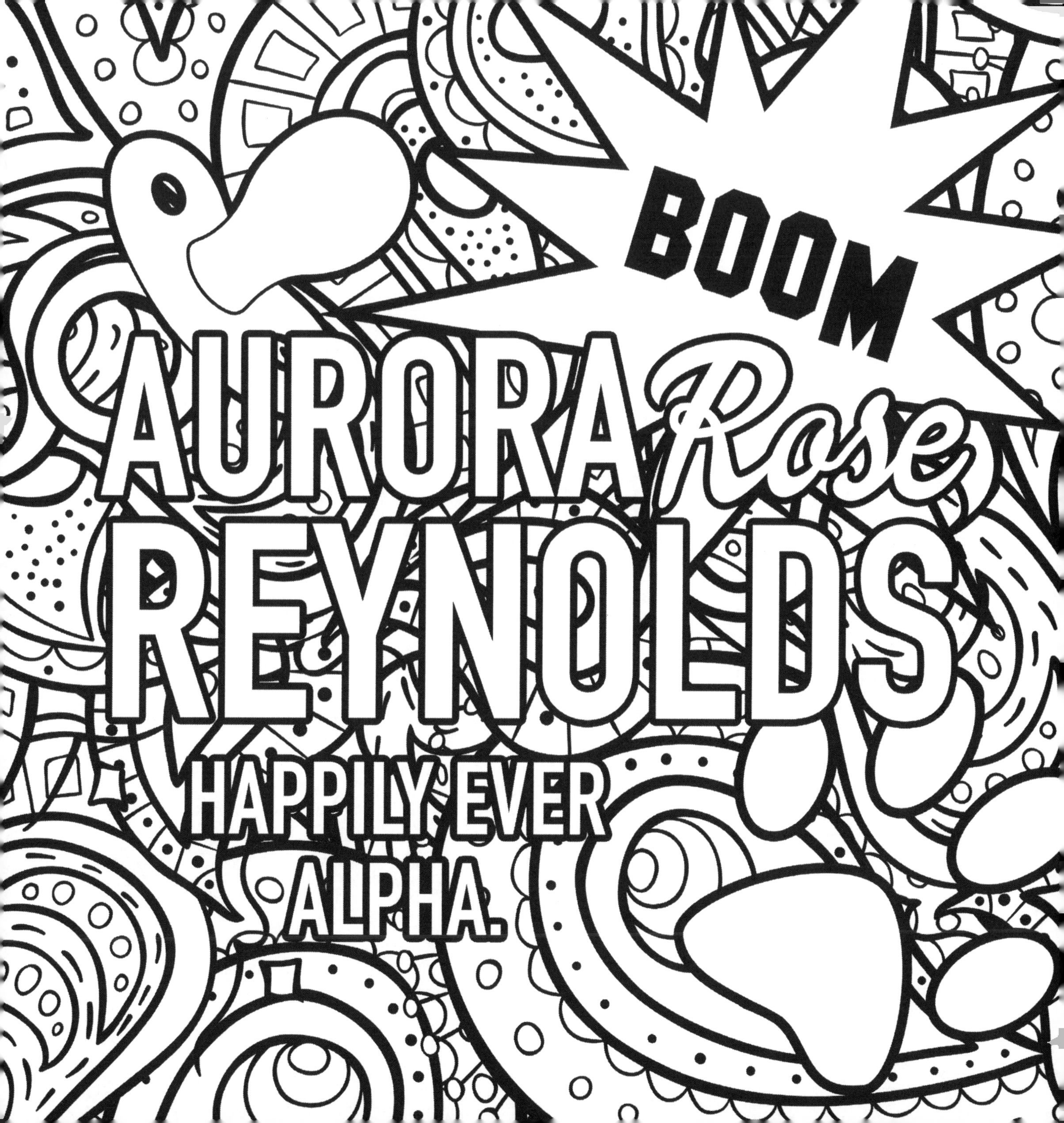
BOOM
AURORA Rose
REYNOLDS
HAPPILY EVER
ALPHA.

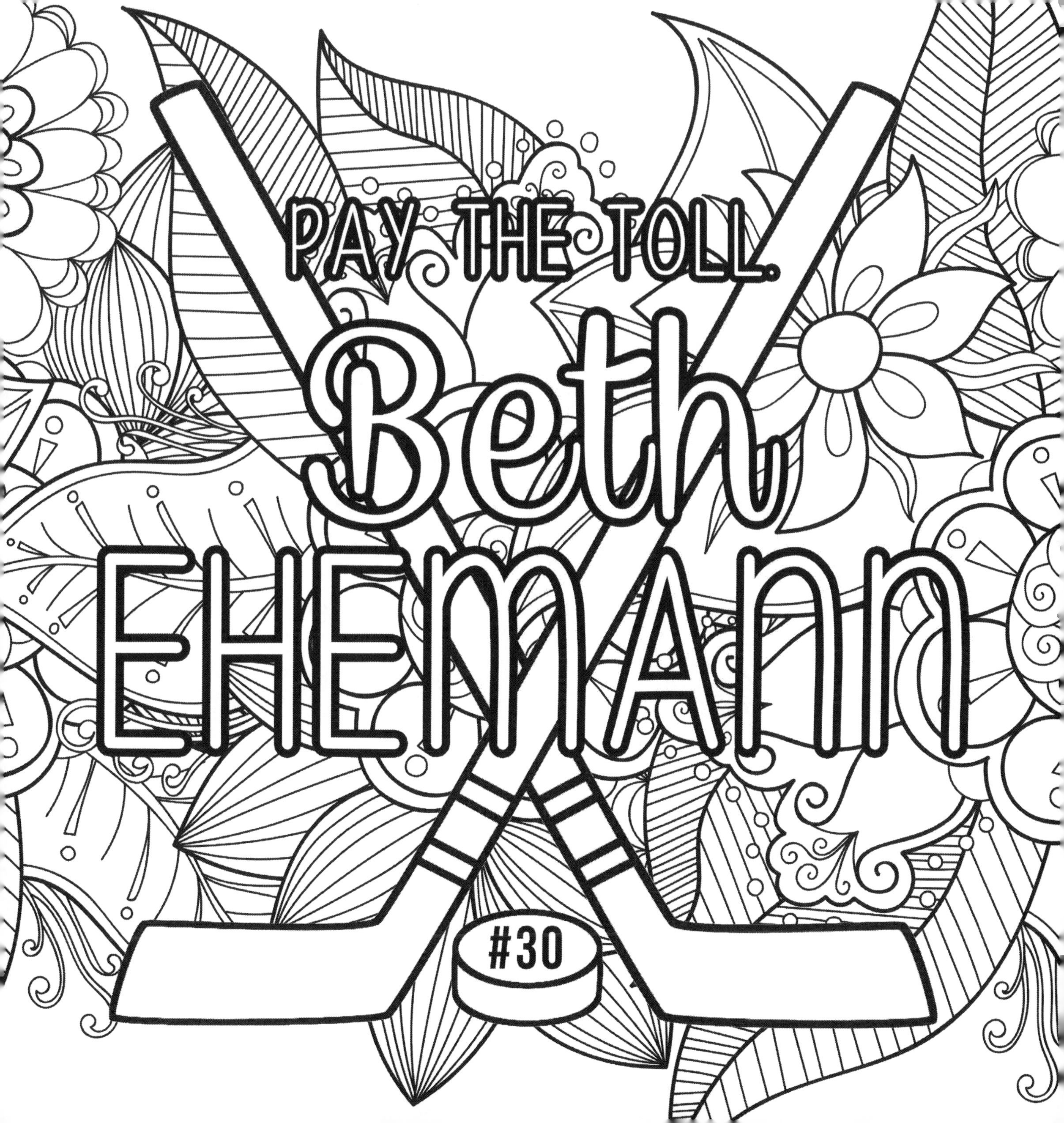
PAY THE TOLL.
Beth
EHEMANN
#30

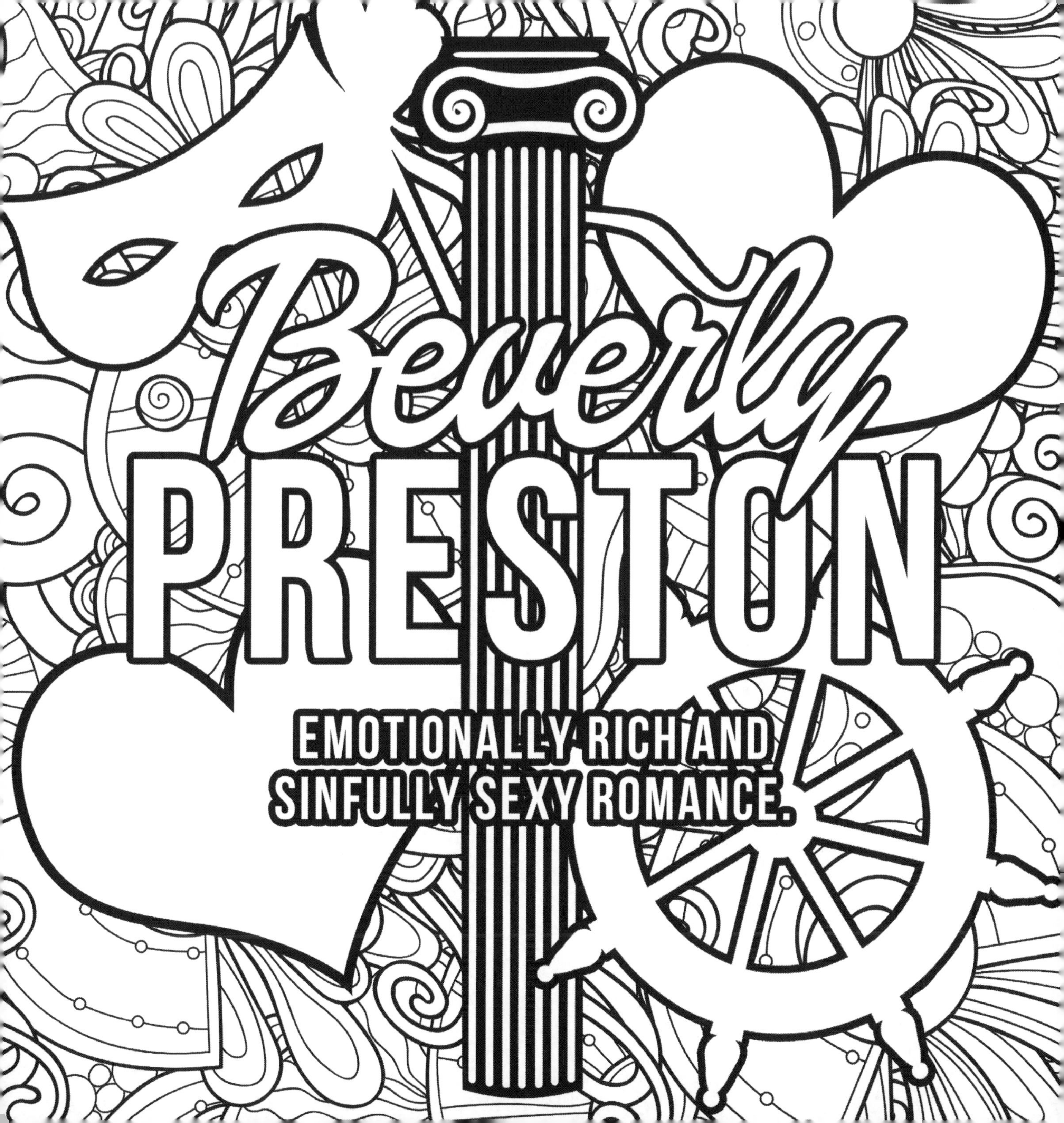
Beverly
PRESTON
EMOTIONALLY RICH AND
SINFULLY SEXY ROMANCE.

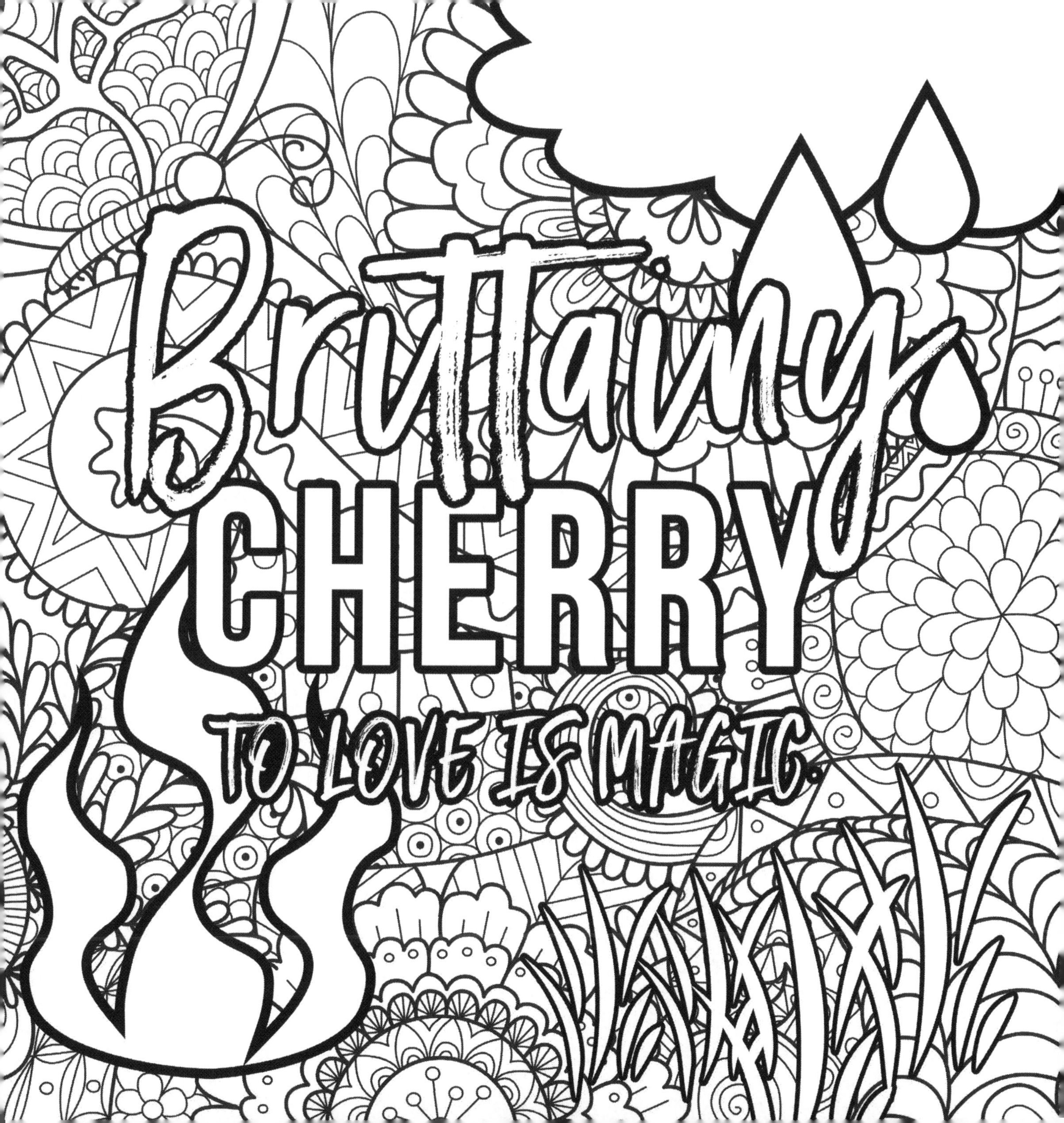
Brittainy
CHERRY
TO LOVE IS MAGIC.

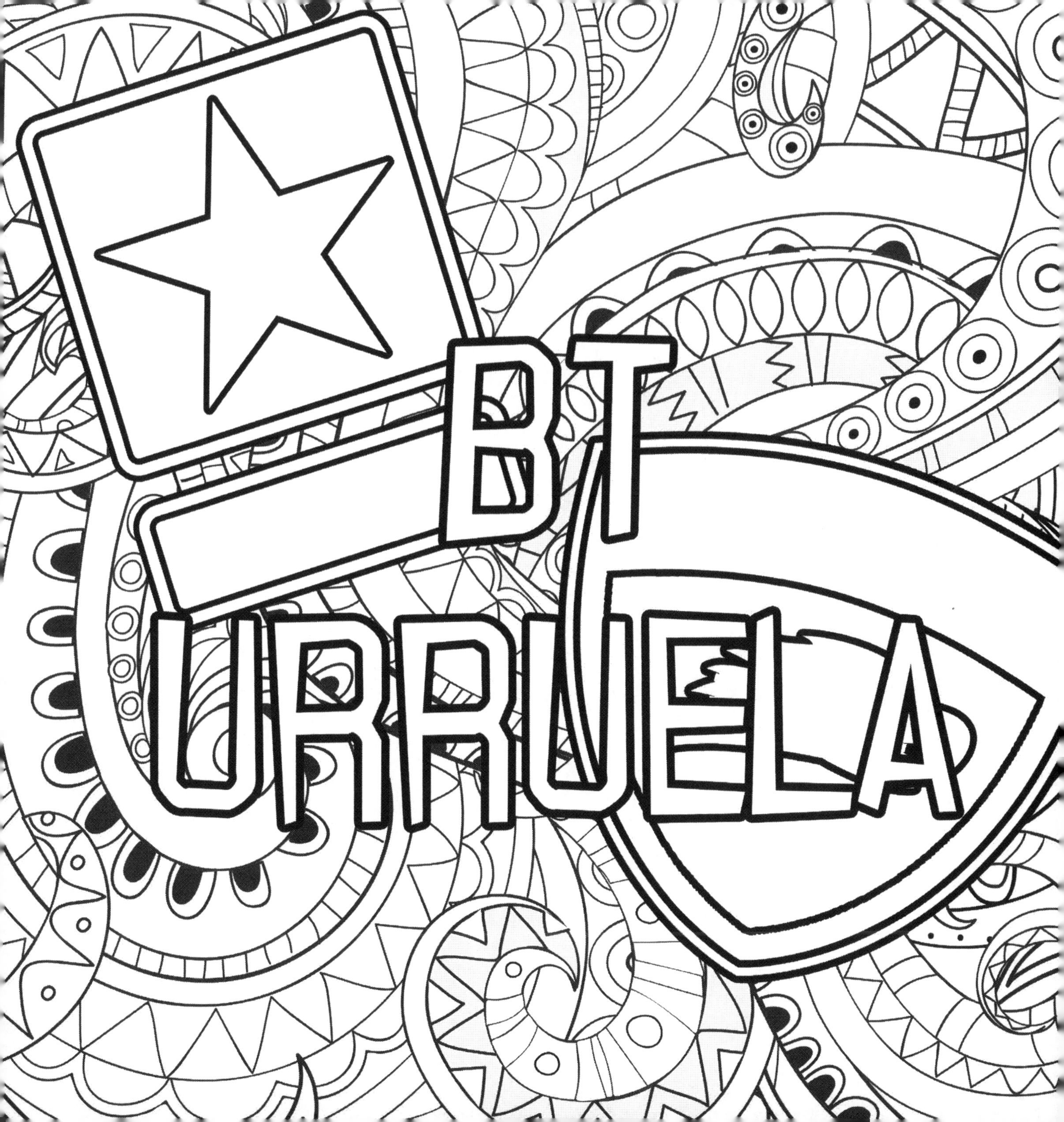
BT
URRUELA

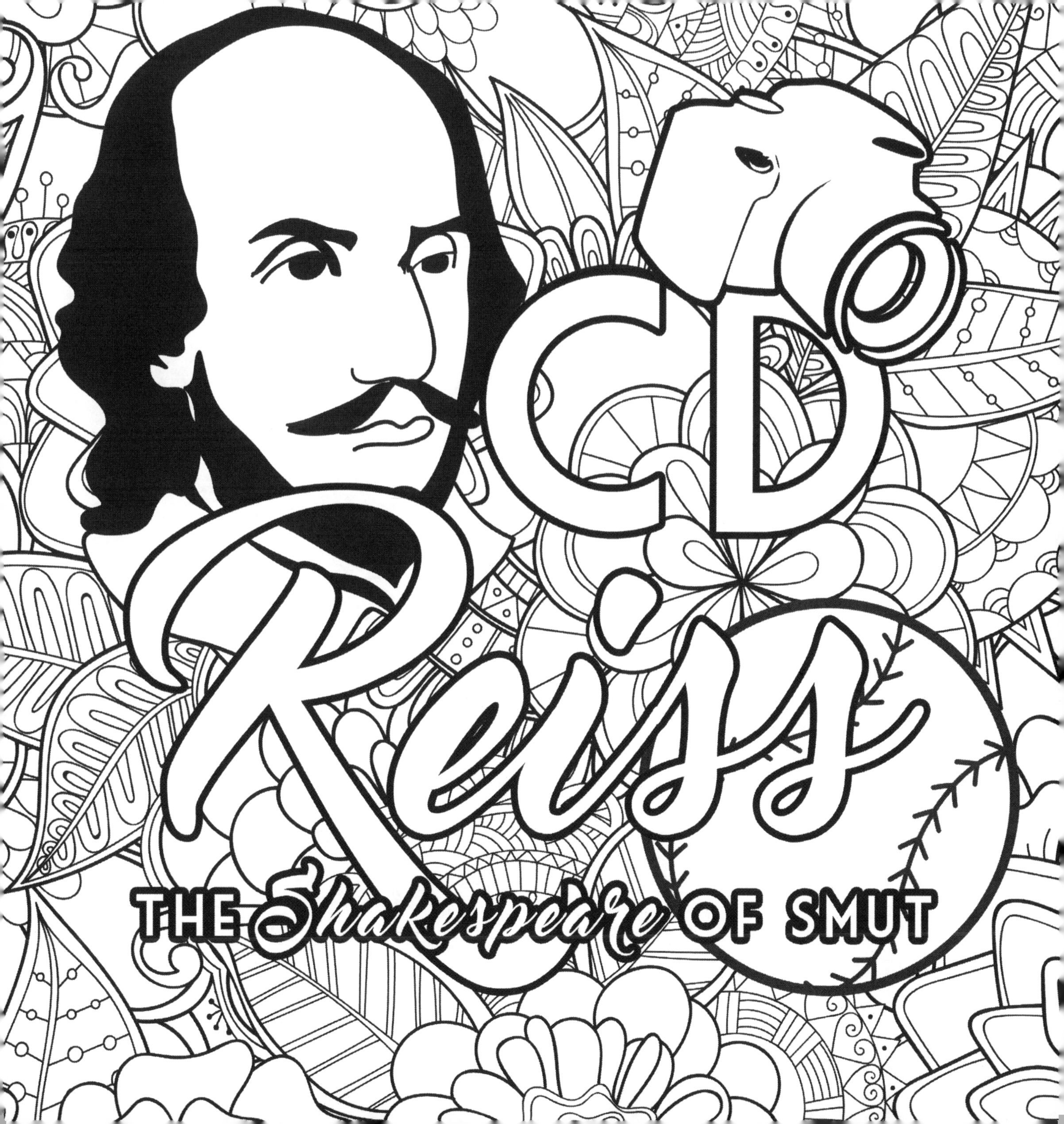
CD
Reiss
THE Shakespeare OF SMUT

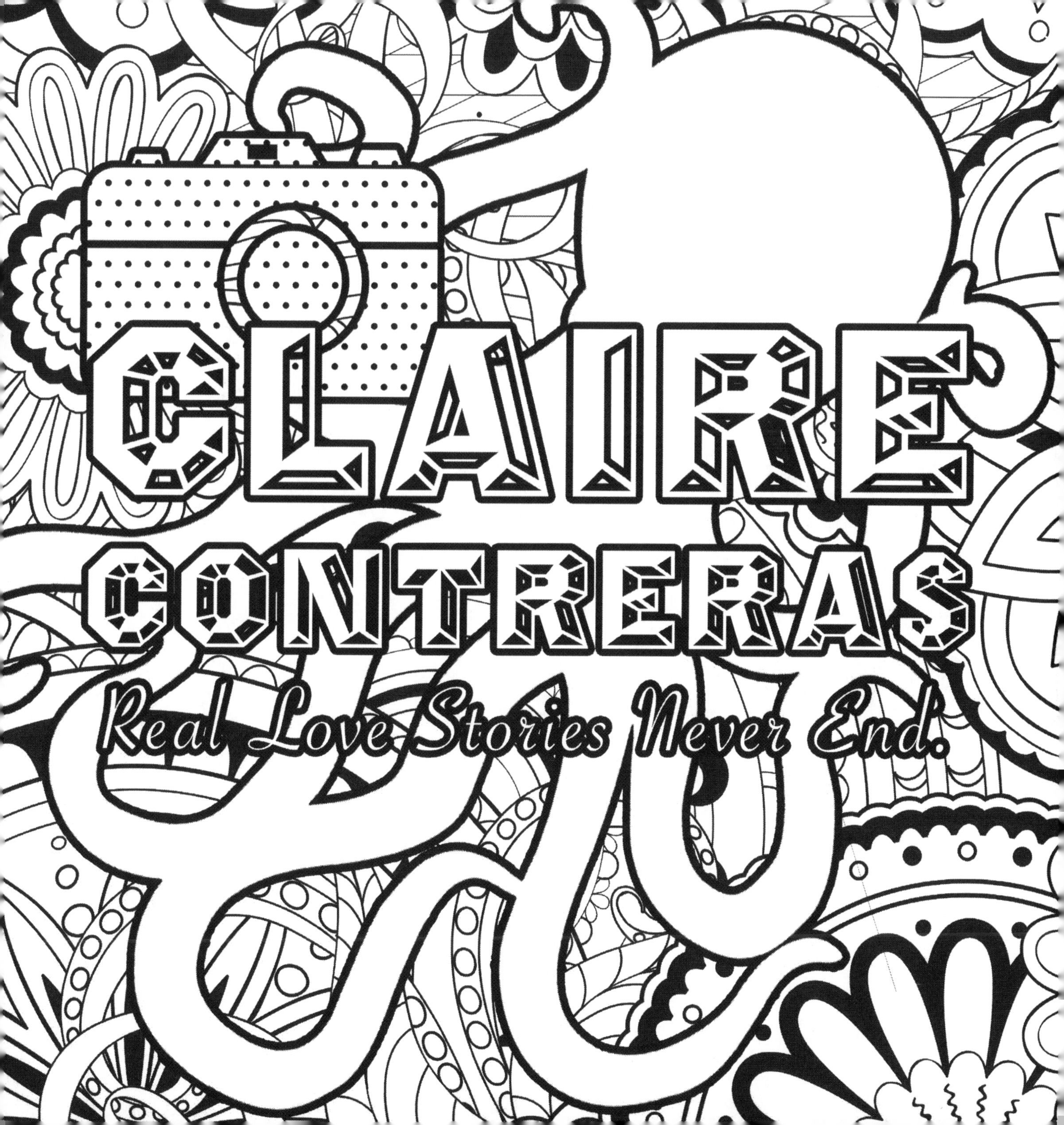
CLAIRE
CONTRERAS
Real Love Stories Never End.

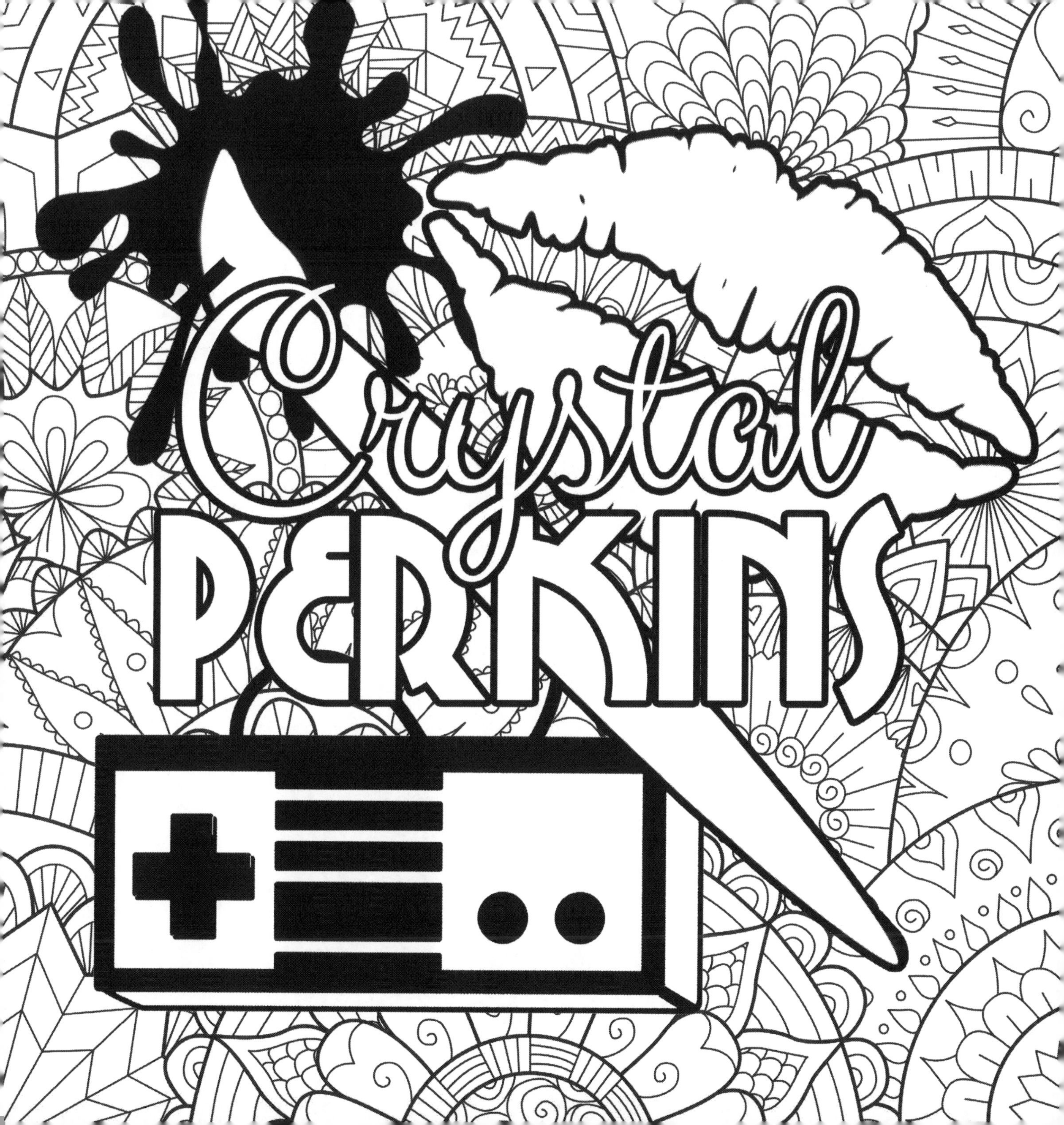
Crystal
PERKINS

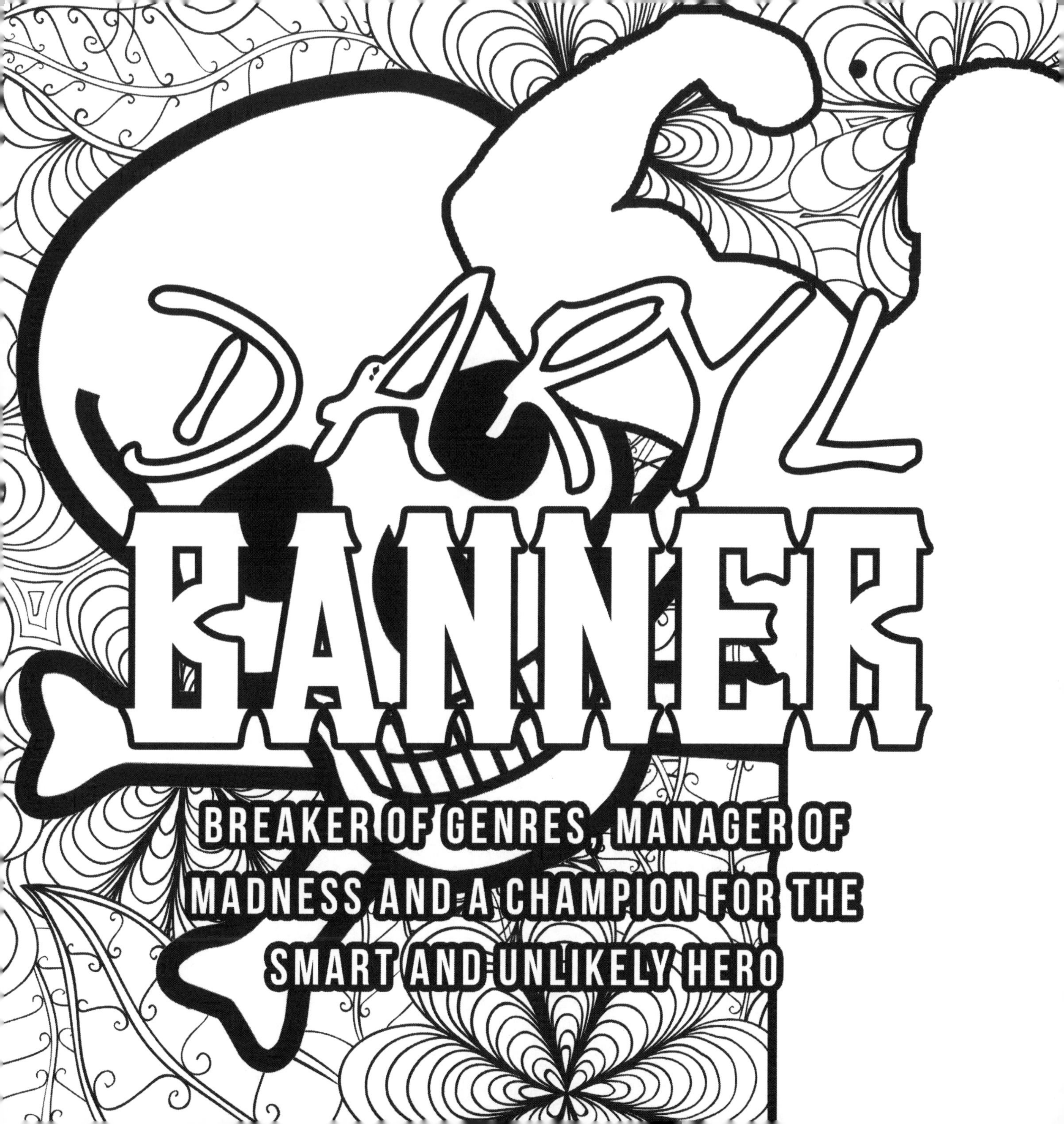
DARYL
BANNER
BREAKER OF GENRES, MANAGER OF MADNESS AND A CHAMPION FOR THE SMART AND UNLIKELY HERO

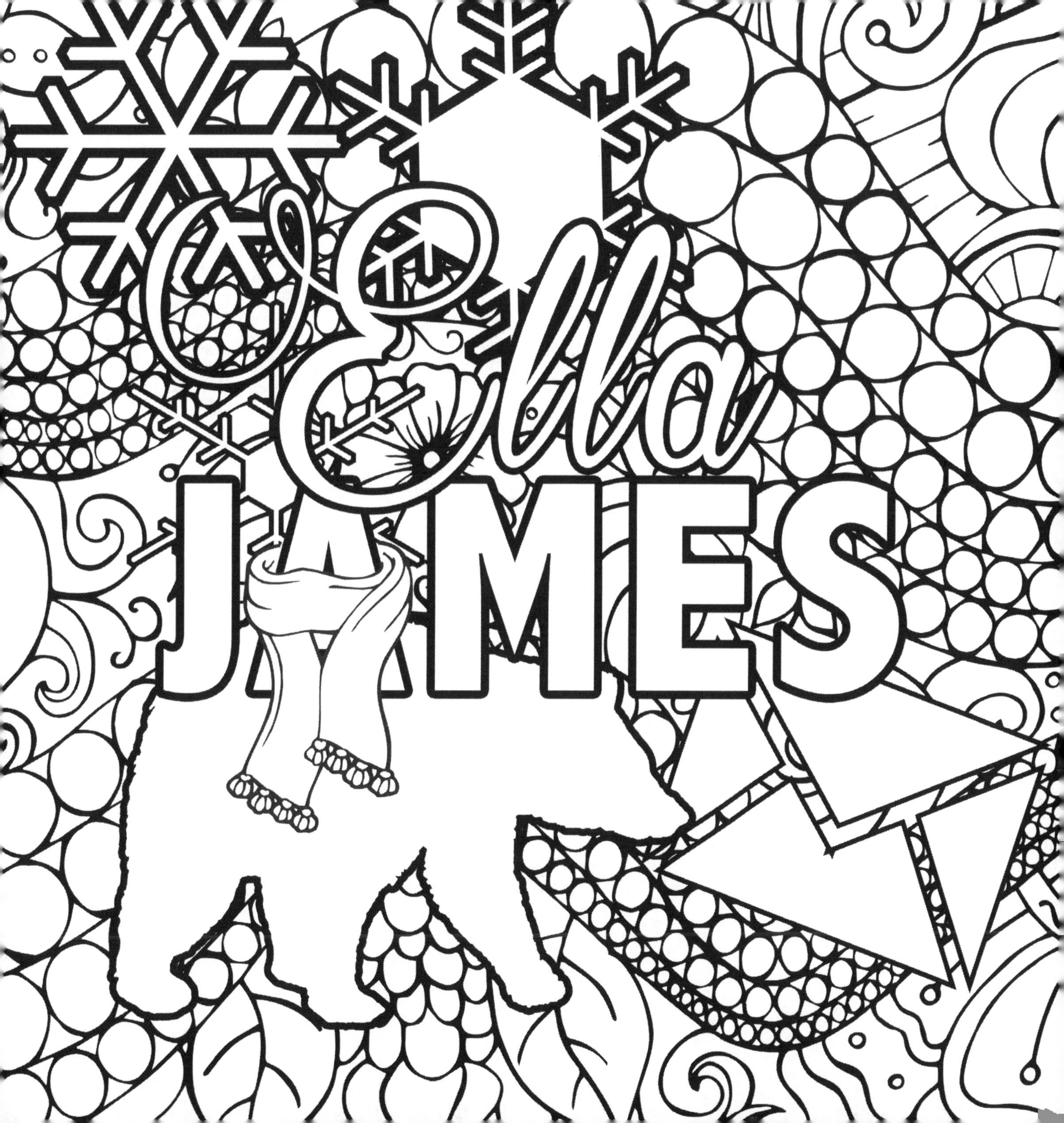
Ella
JAMES

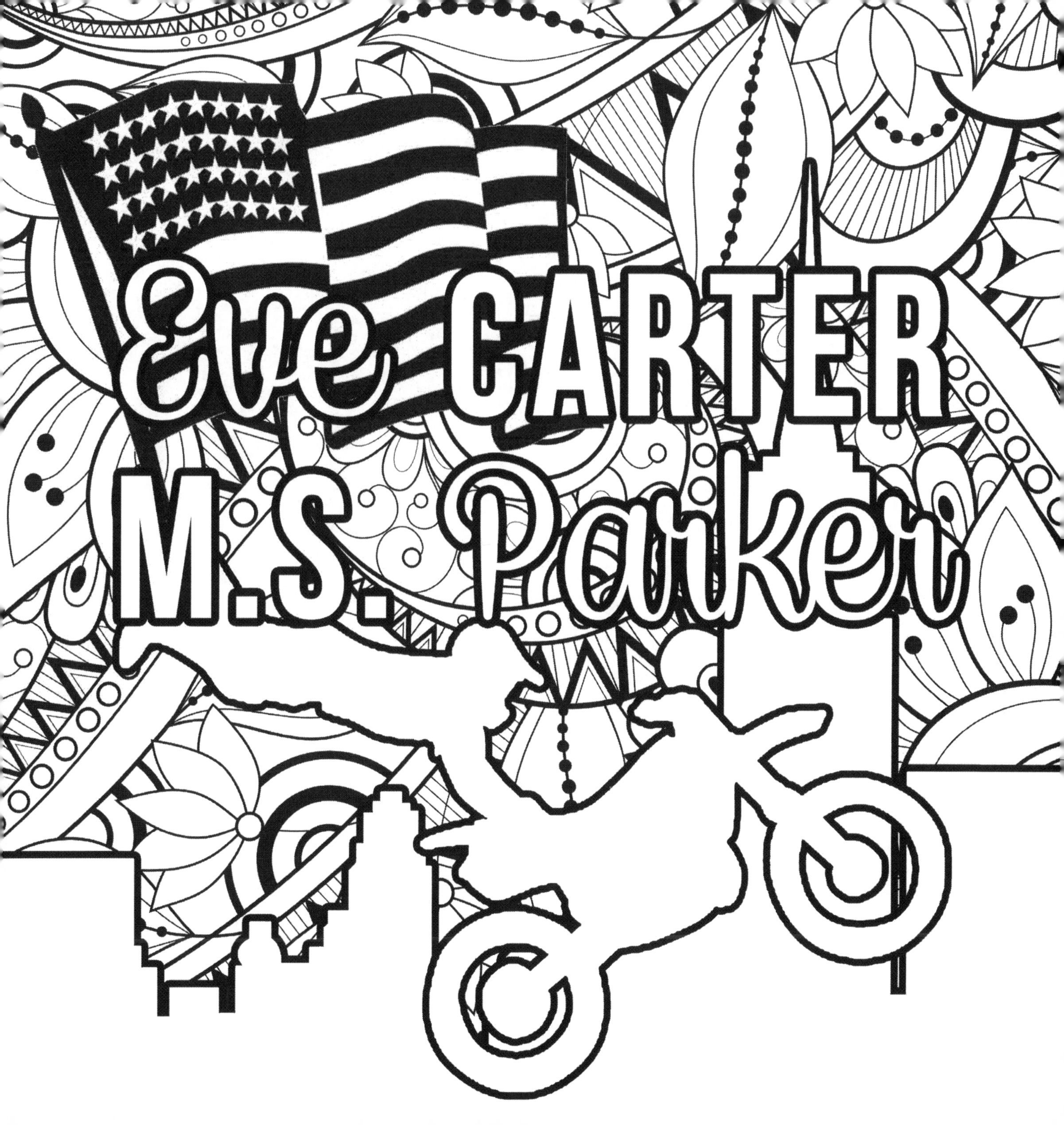
Eve CARTER
M.S. Parker

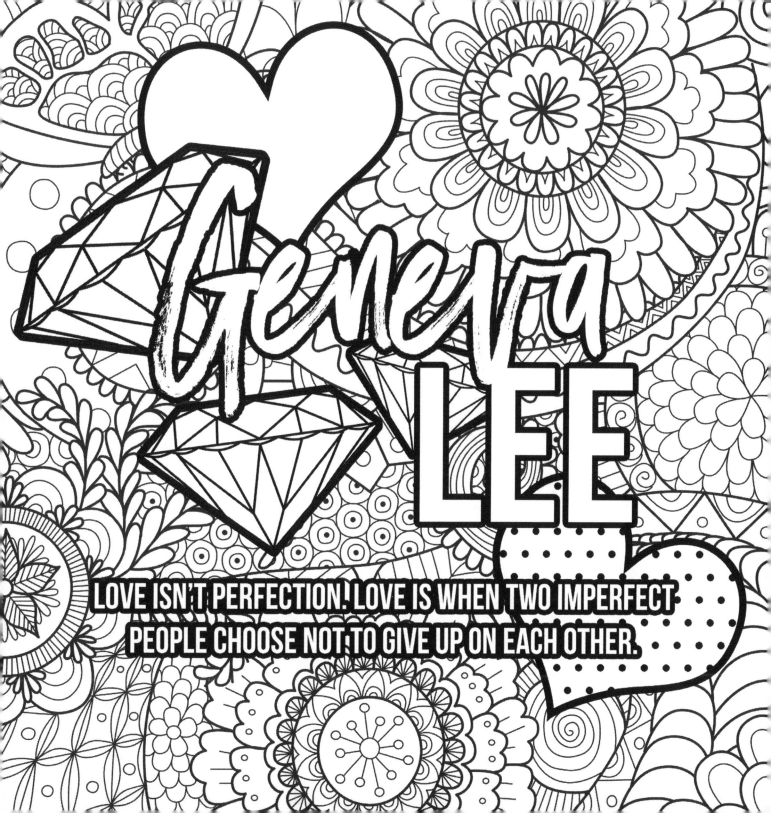

Geneva LEE

LOVE ISN'T PERFECTION! LOVE IS WHEN TWO IMPERFECT PEOPLE CHOOSE NOT TO GIVE UP ON EACH OTHER.

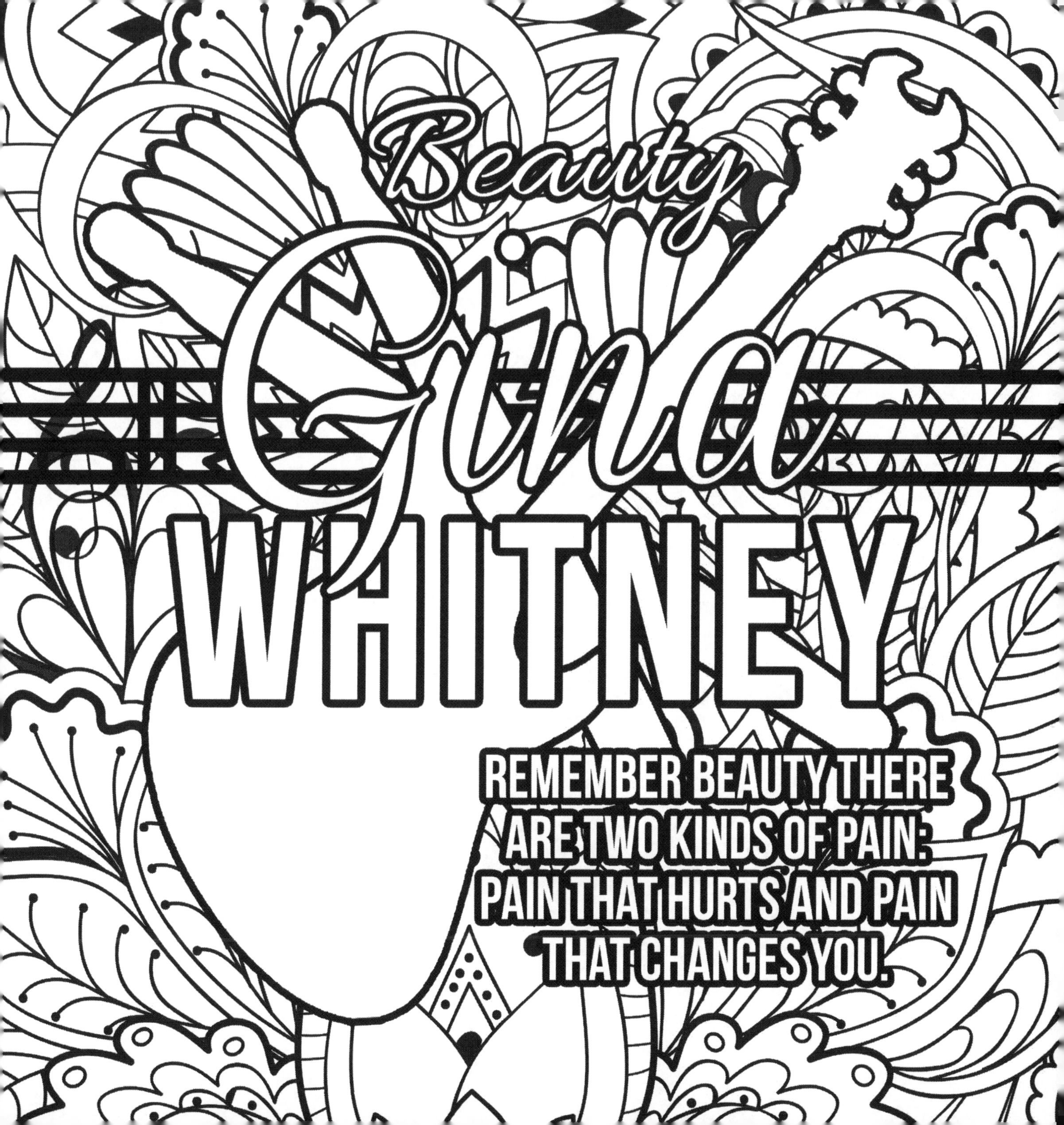
Beauty
Gina
WHITNEY
REMEMBER BEAUTY THERE ARE TWO KINDS OF PAIN: PAIN THAT HURTS AND PAIN THAT CHANGES YOU.

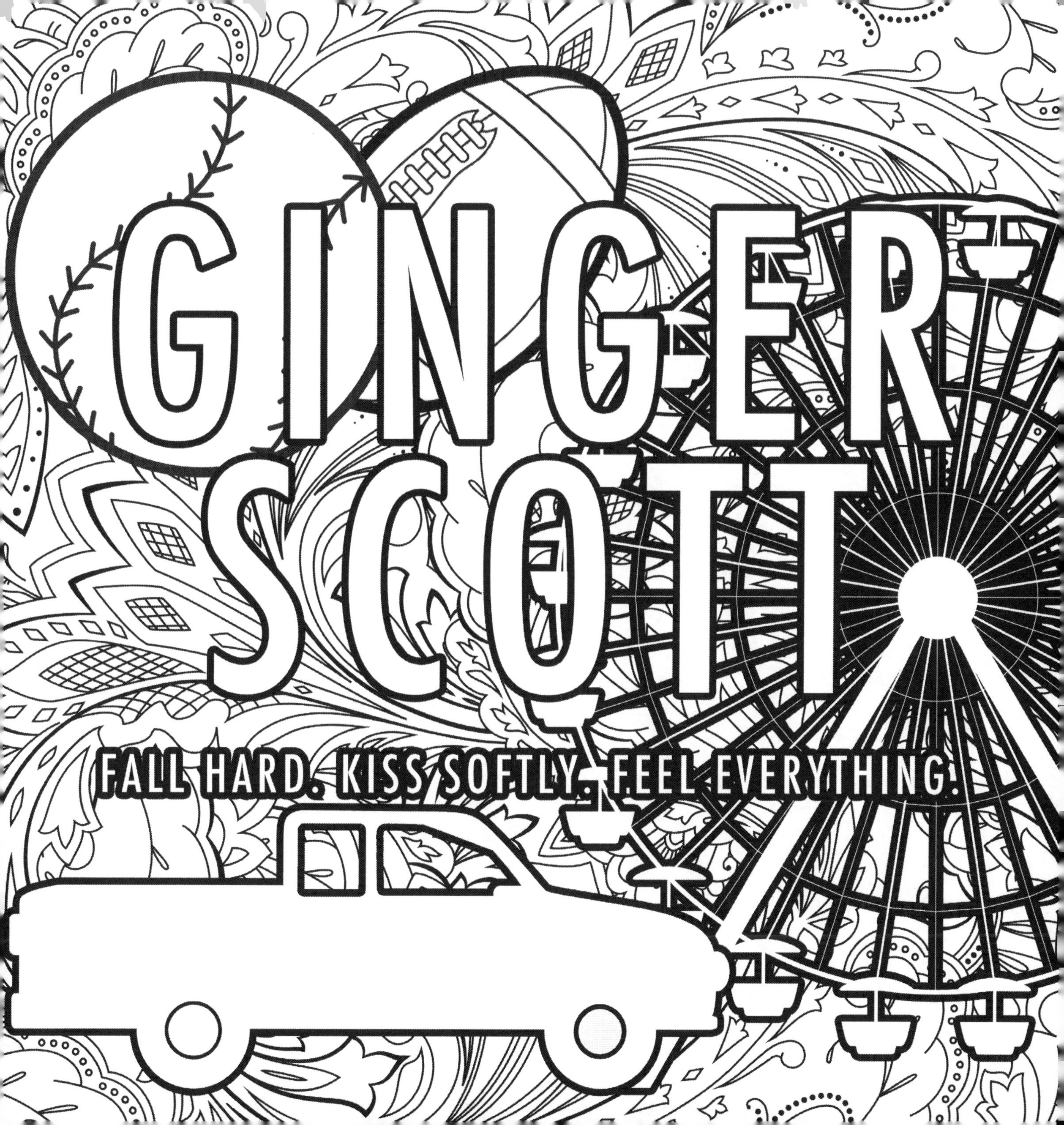
GINGER
SCOTT
FALL HARD. KISS SOFTLY. FEEL EVERYTHING.

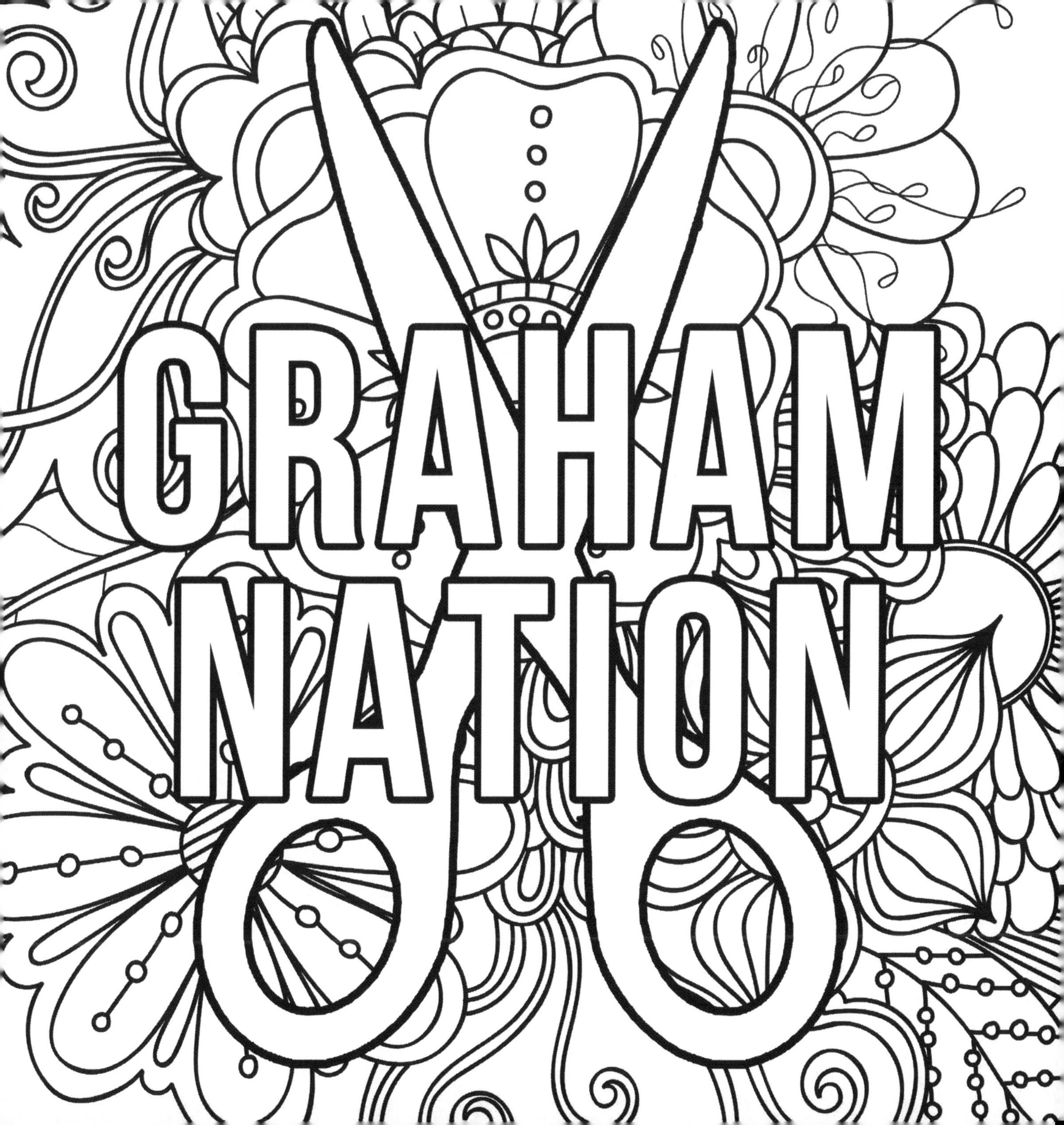
GRAHAM
NATION

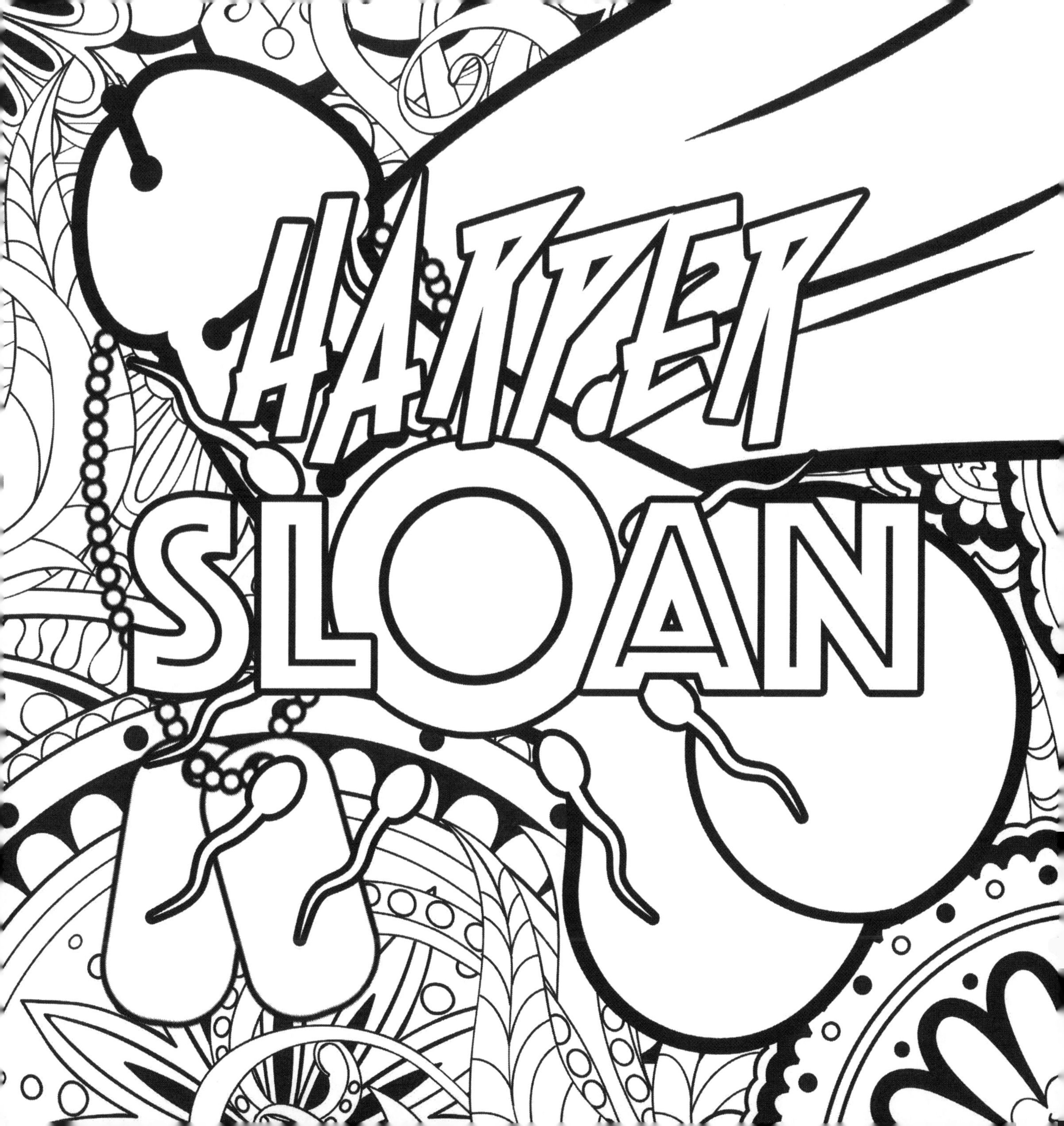
HARPER
SLOAN

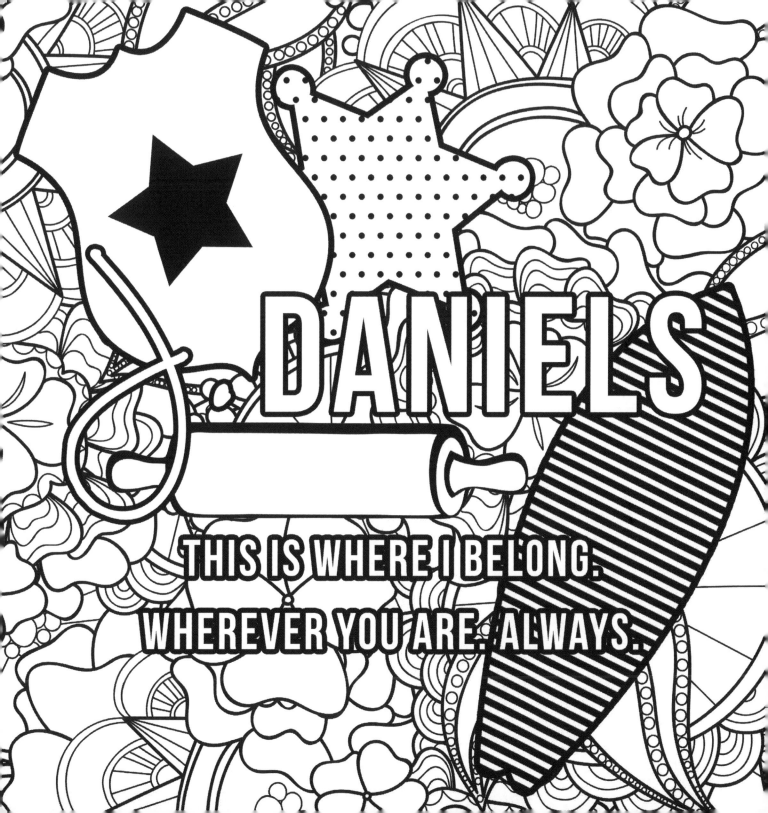

DANIELS

THIS IS WHERE I BELONG.

WHEREVER YOU ARE. ALWAYS.

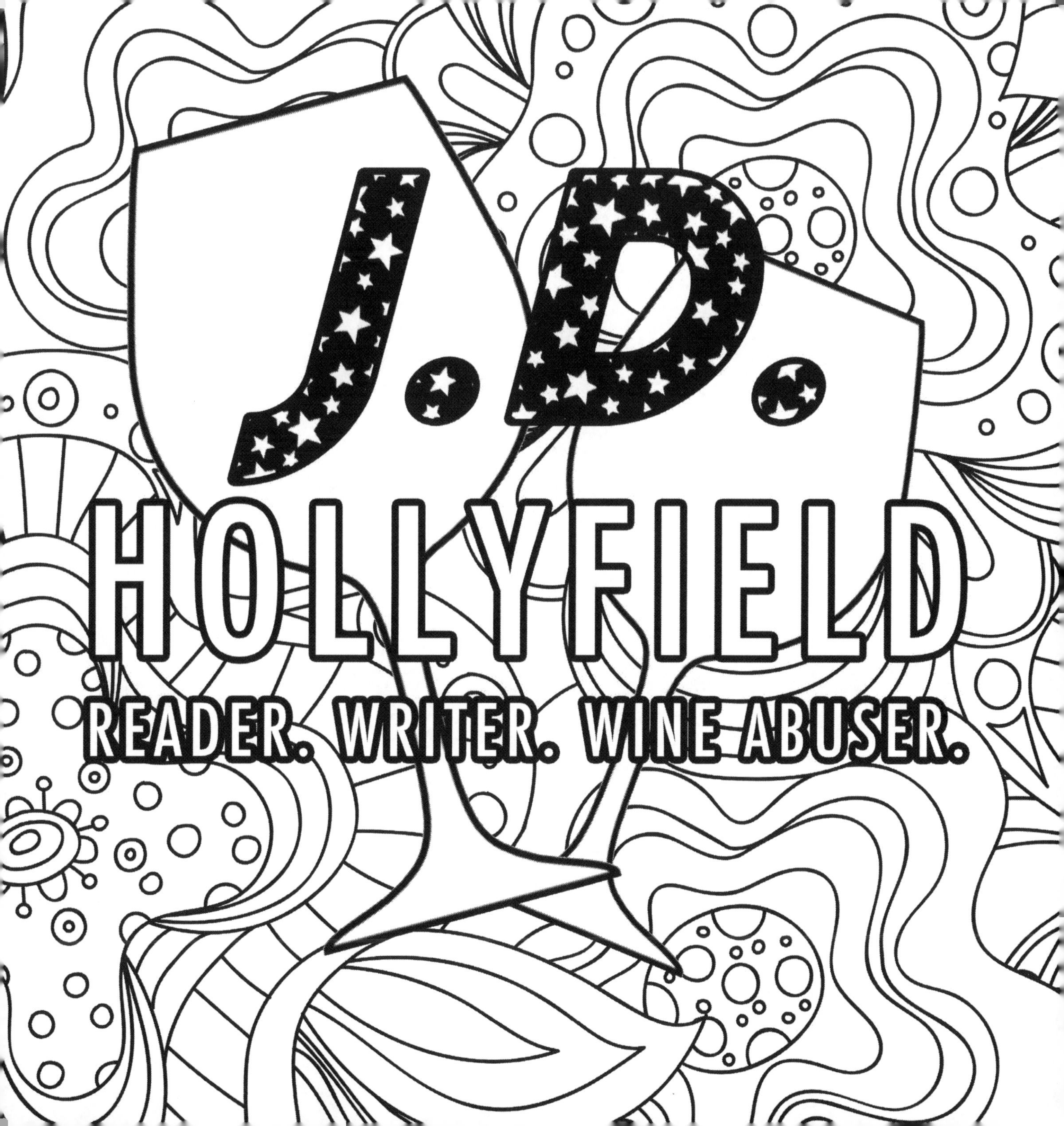
J.D.
HOLLYFIELD
READER. WRITER. WINE ABUSER.

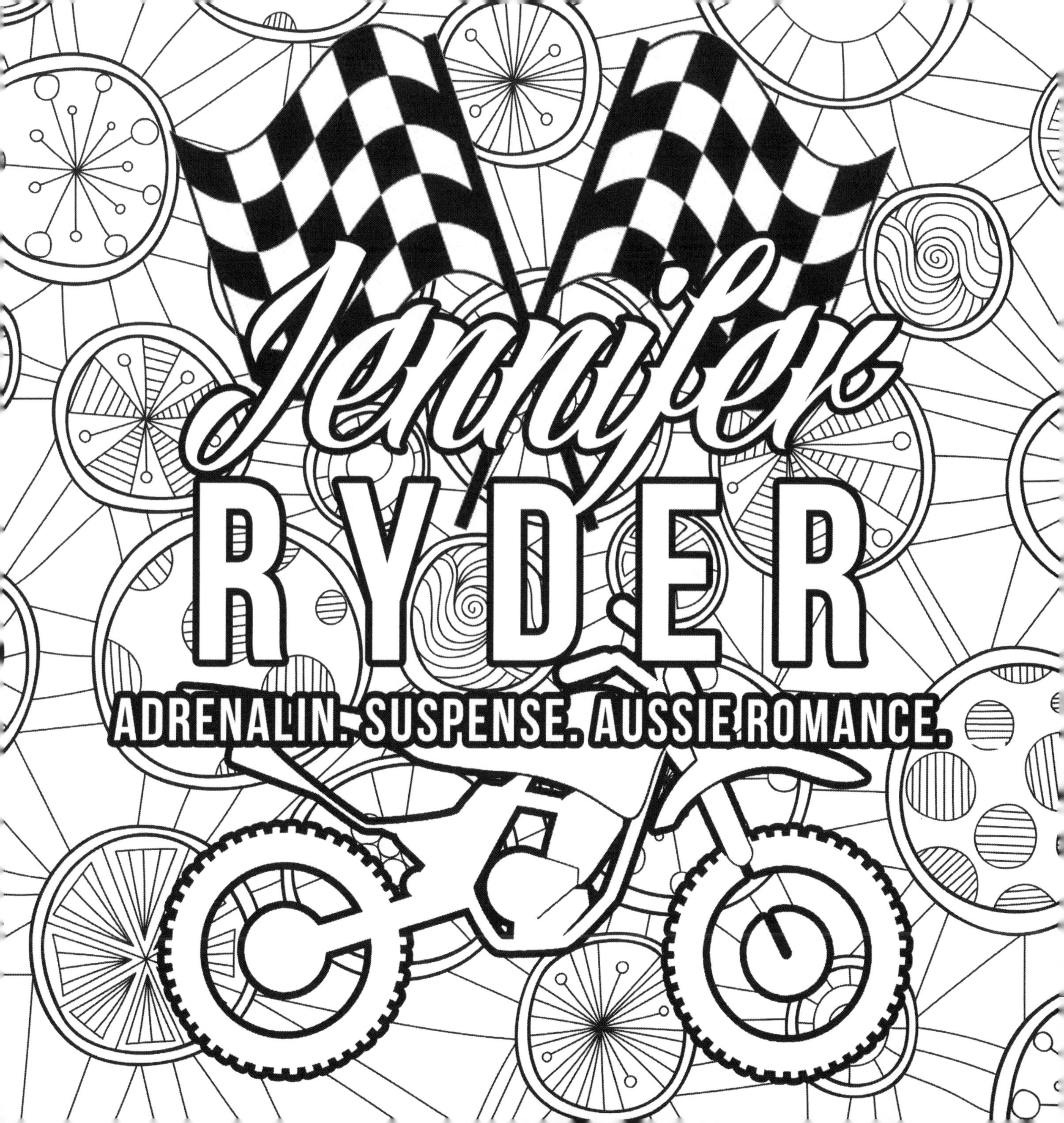
Jennifer
RYDER
ADRENALIN. SUSPENSE. AUSSIE ROMANCE.

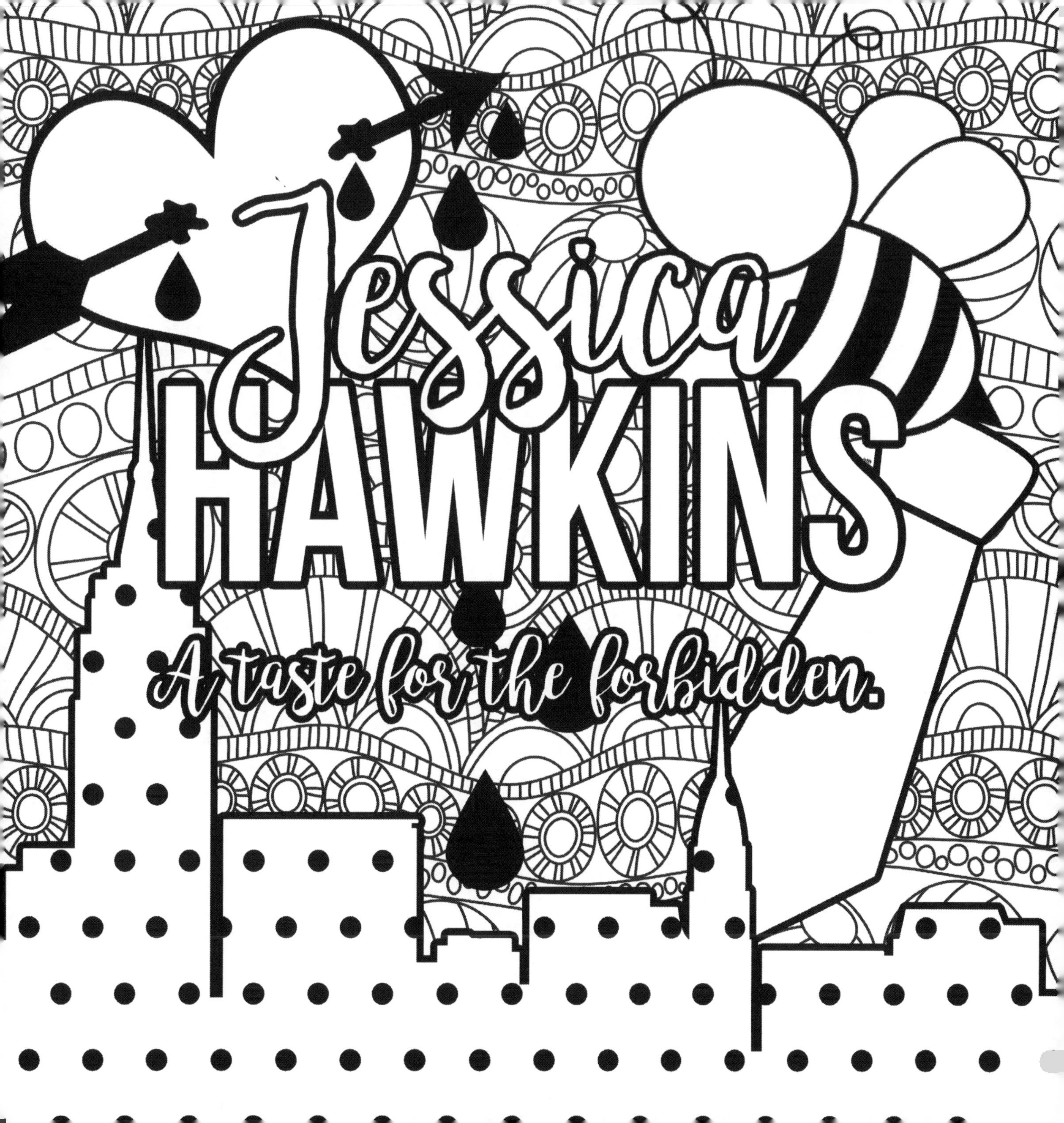
Jessica
HAWKINS
A taste for the forbidden.

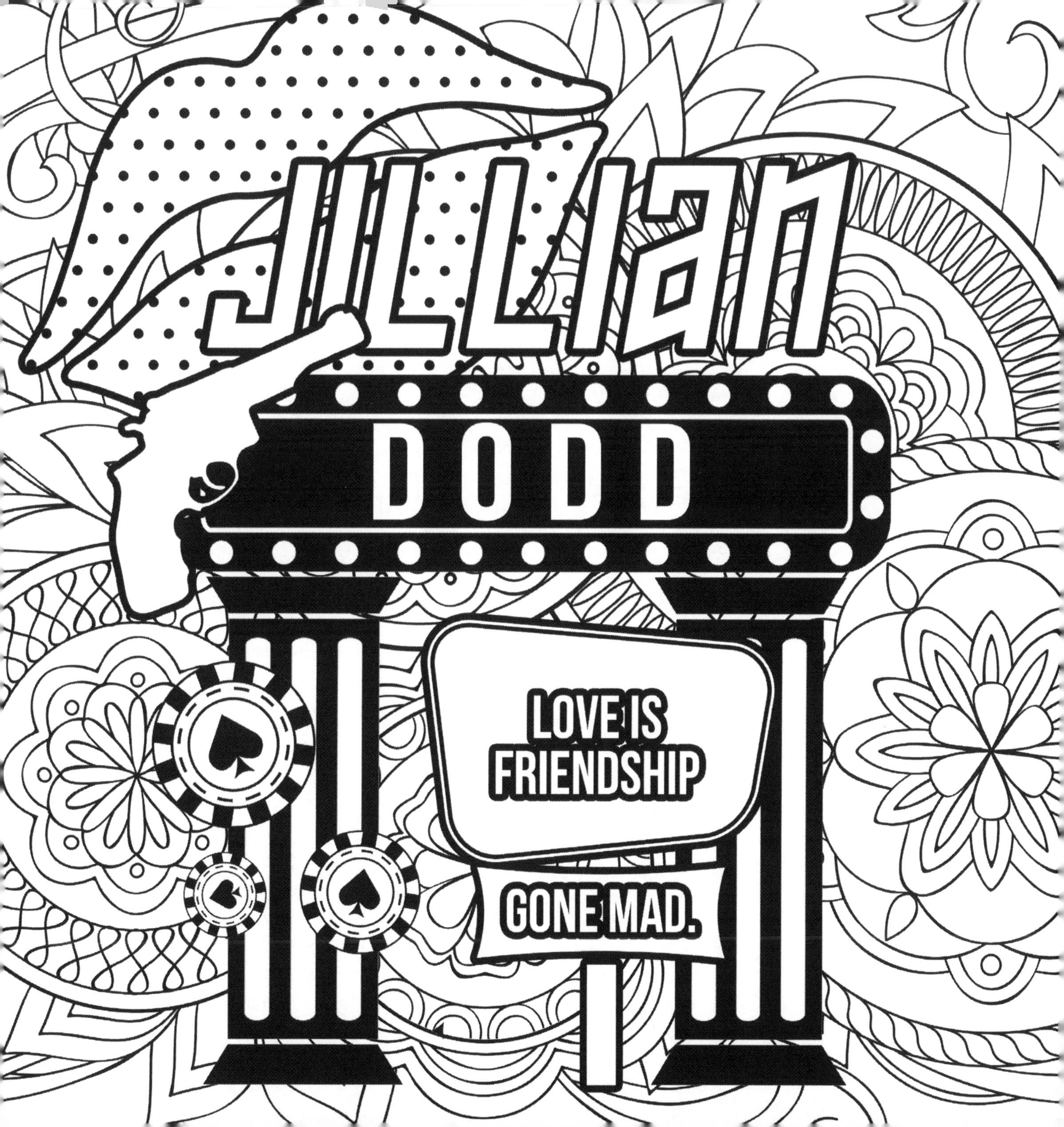
JILLIAN
DODD
LOVE IS
FRIENDSHIP
GONE MAD.

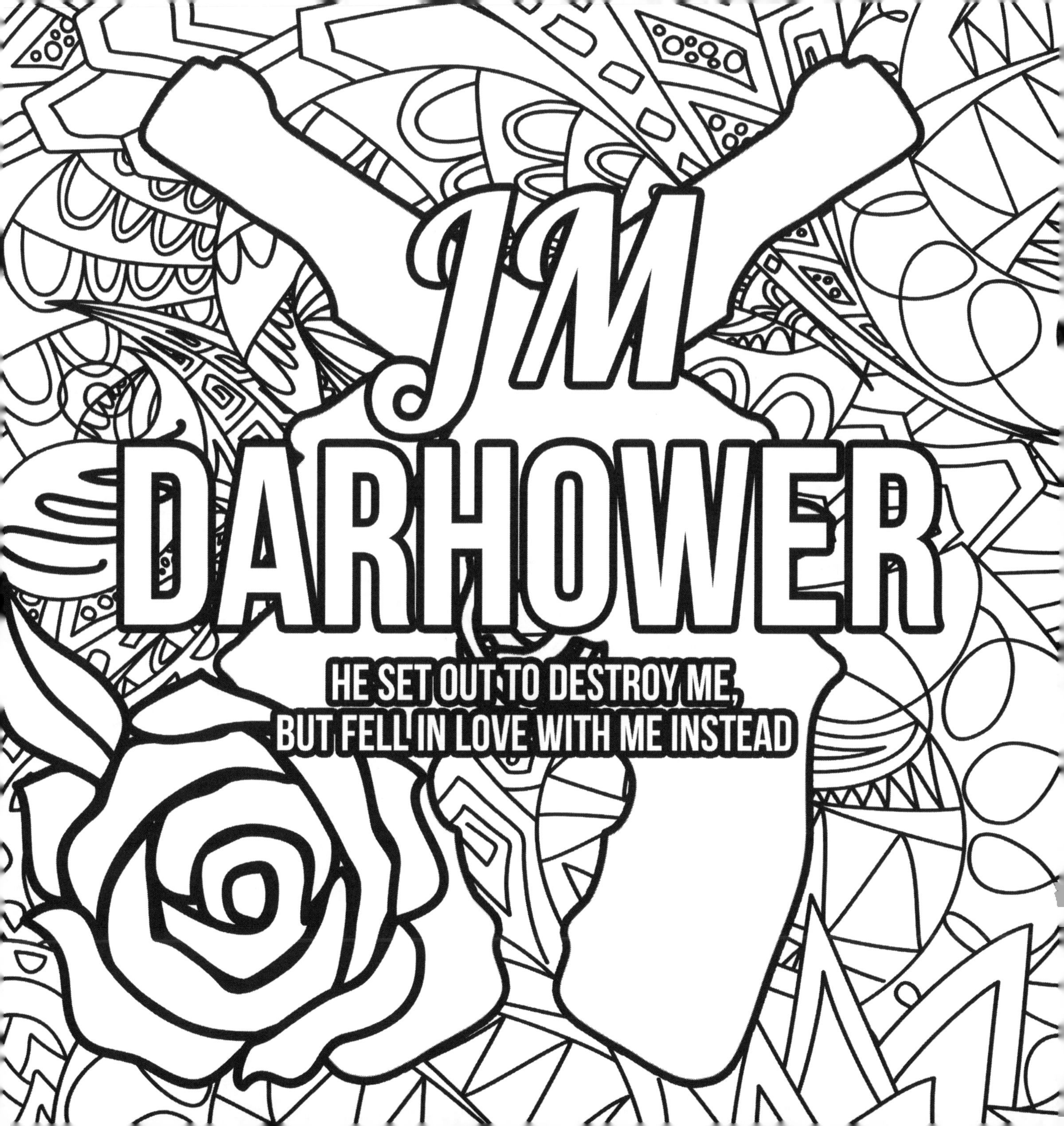
JM
DARHOWER
HE SET OUT TO DESTROY ME,
BUT FELL IN LOVE WITH ME INSTEAD

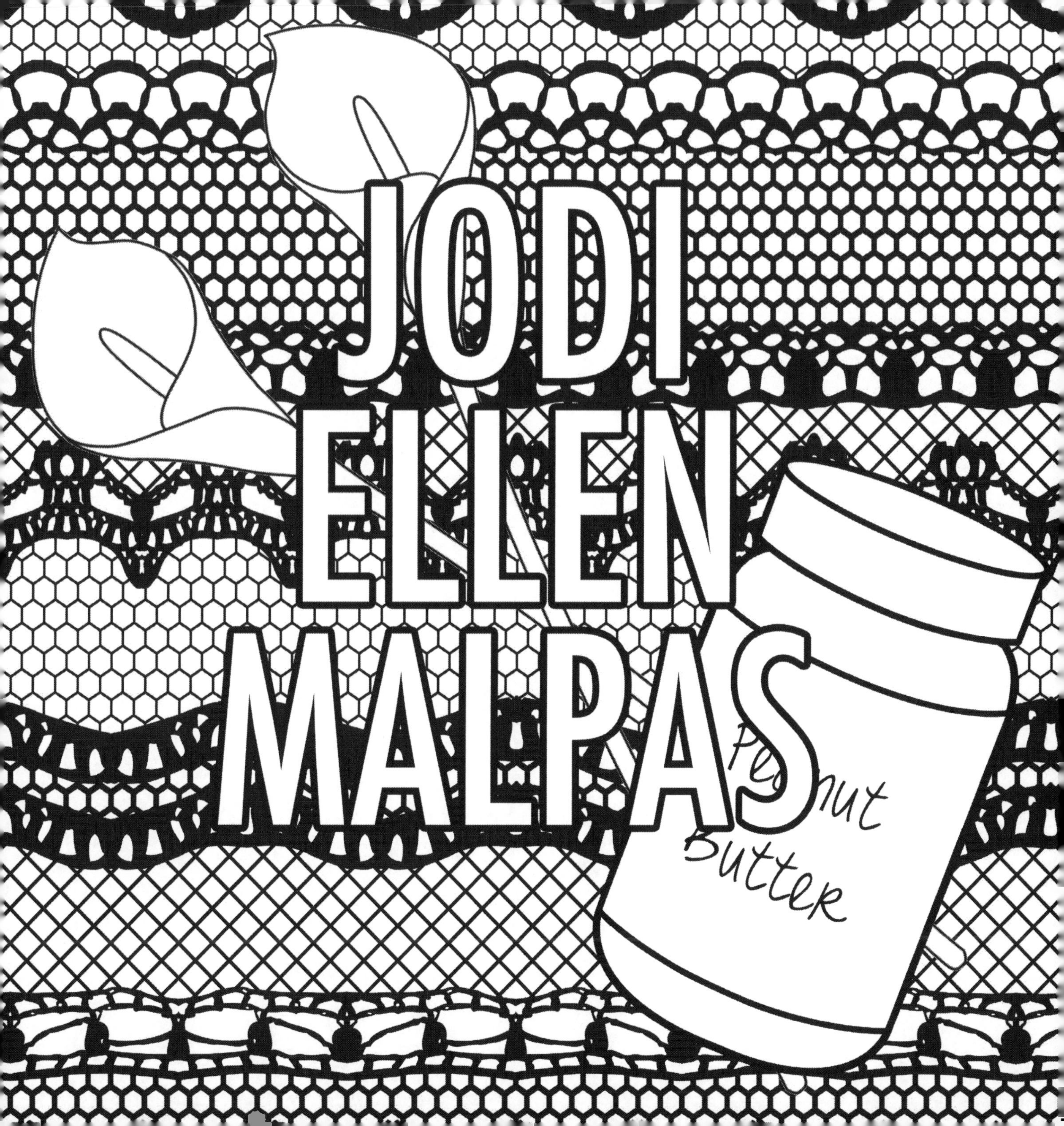
JODI
ELLEN
MALPAS
Butter

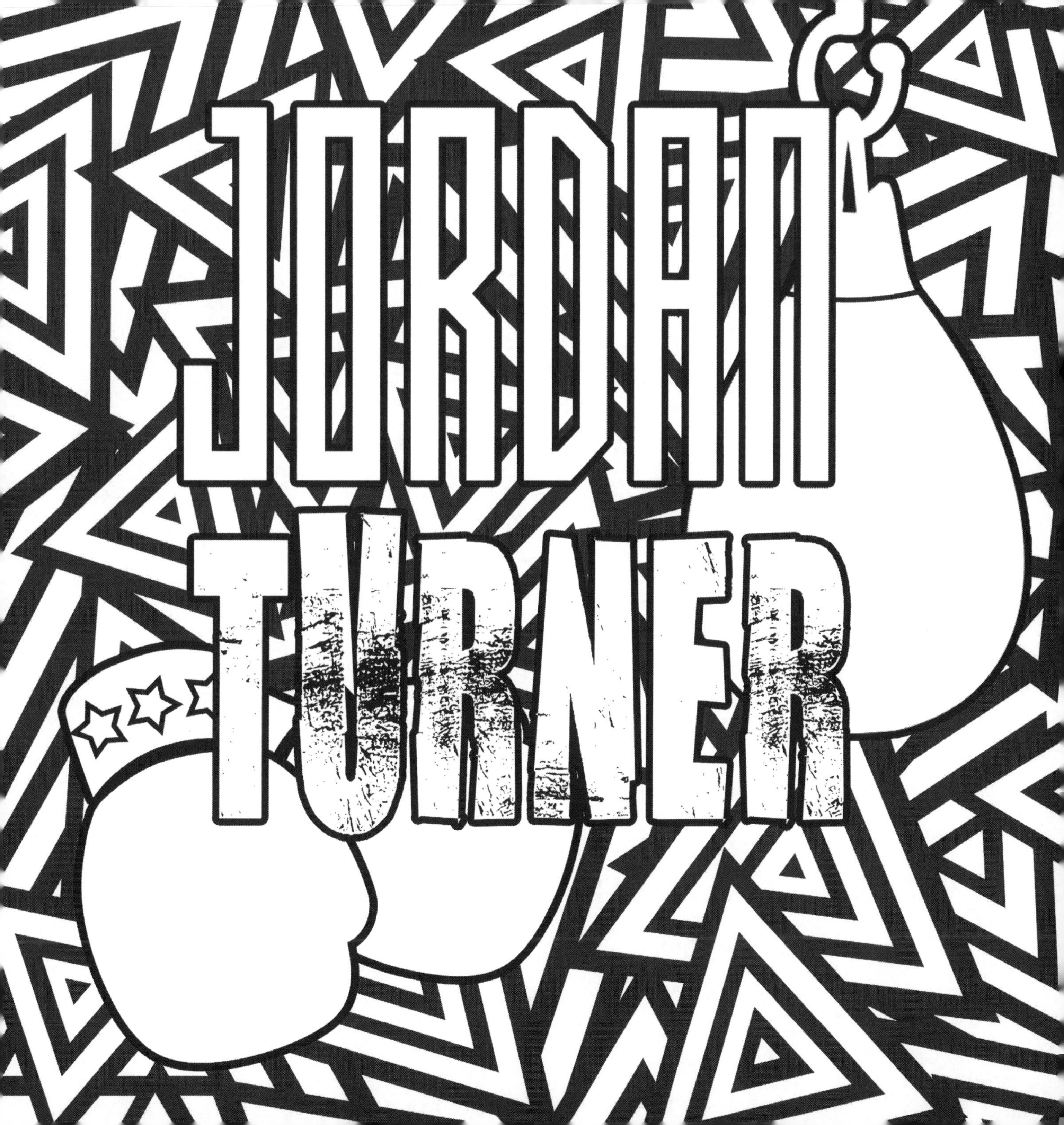
JORDAN
TURNER

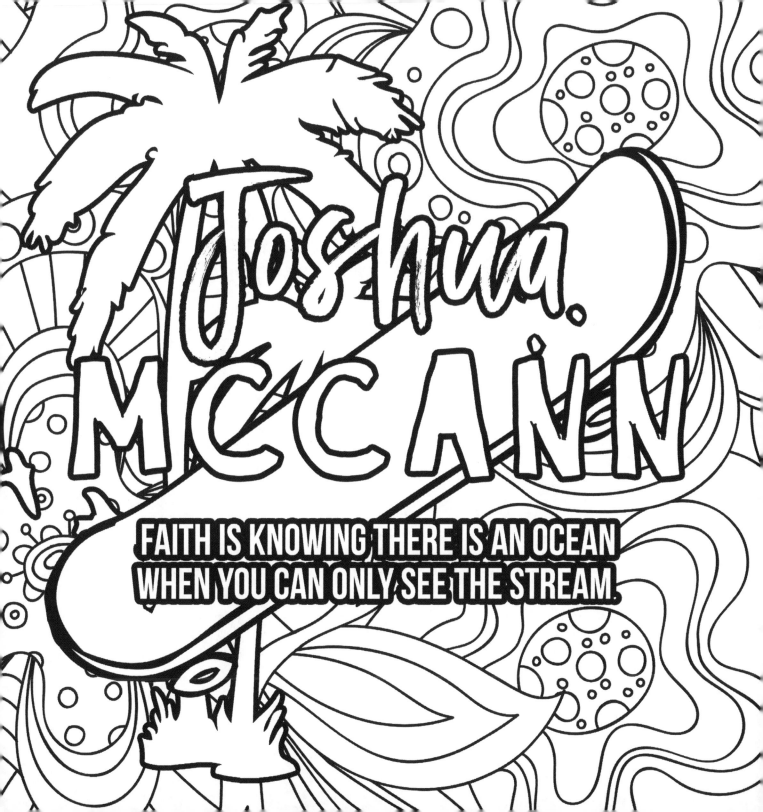

Joshua McCann

FAITH IS KNOWING THERE IS AN OCEAN
WHEN YOU CAN ONLY SEE THE STREAM.

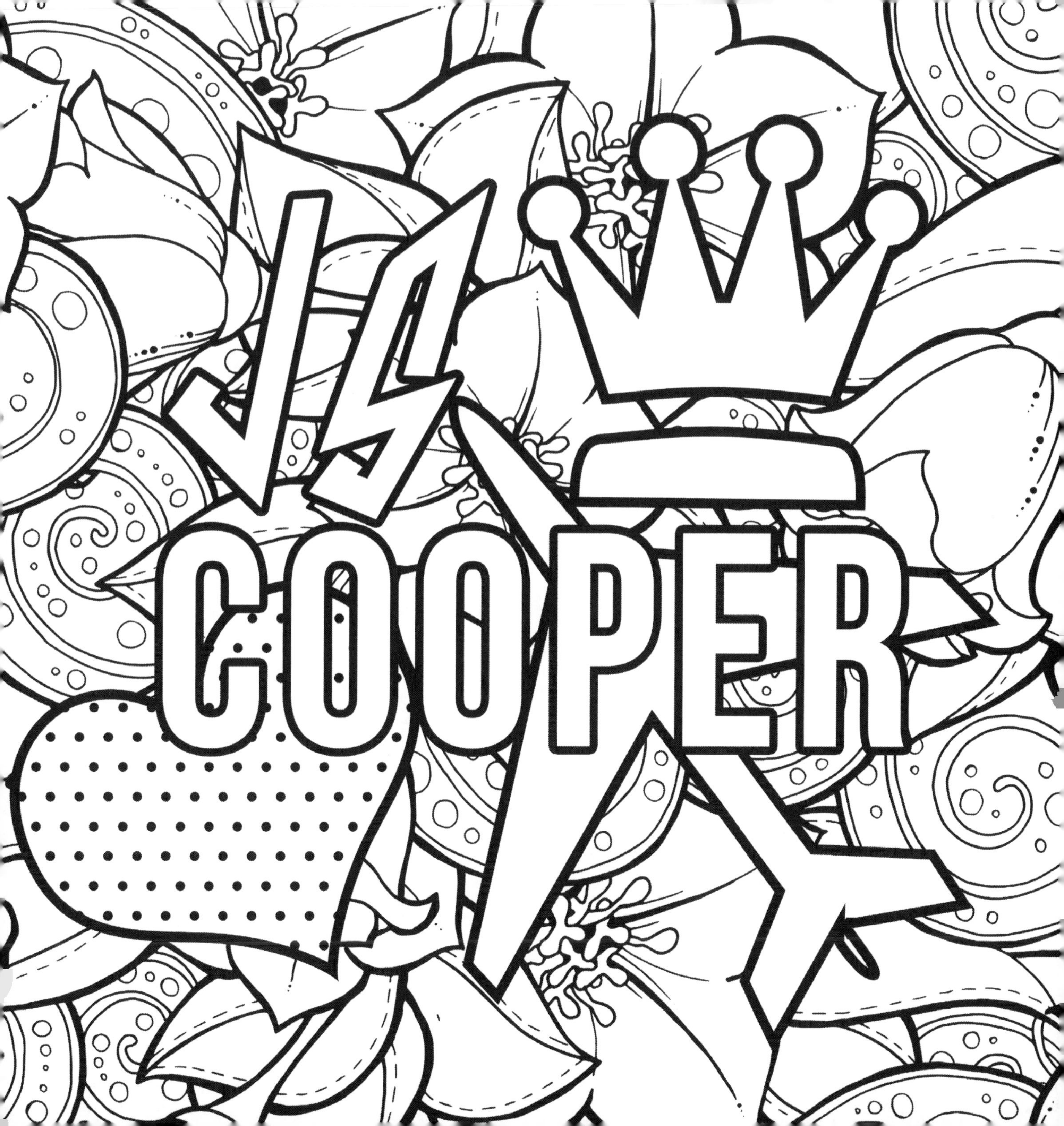
COOPER

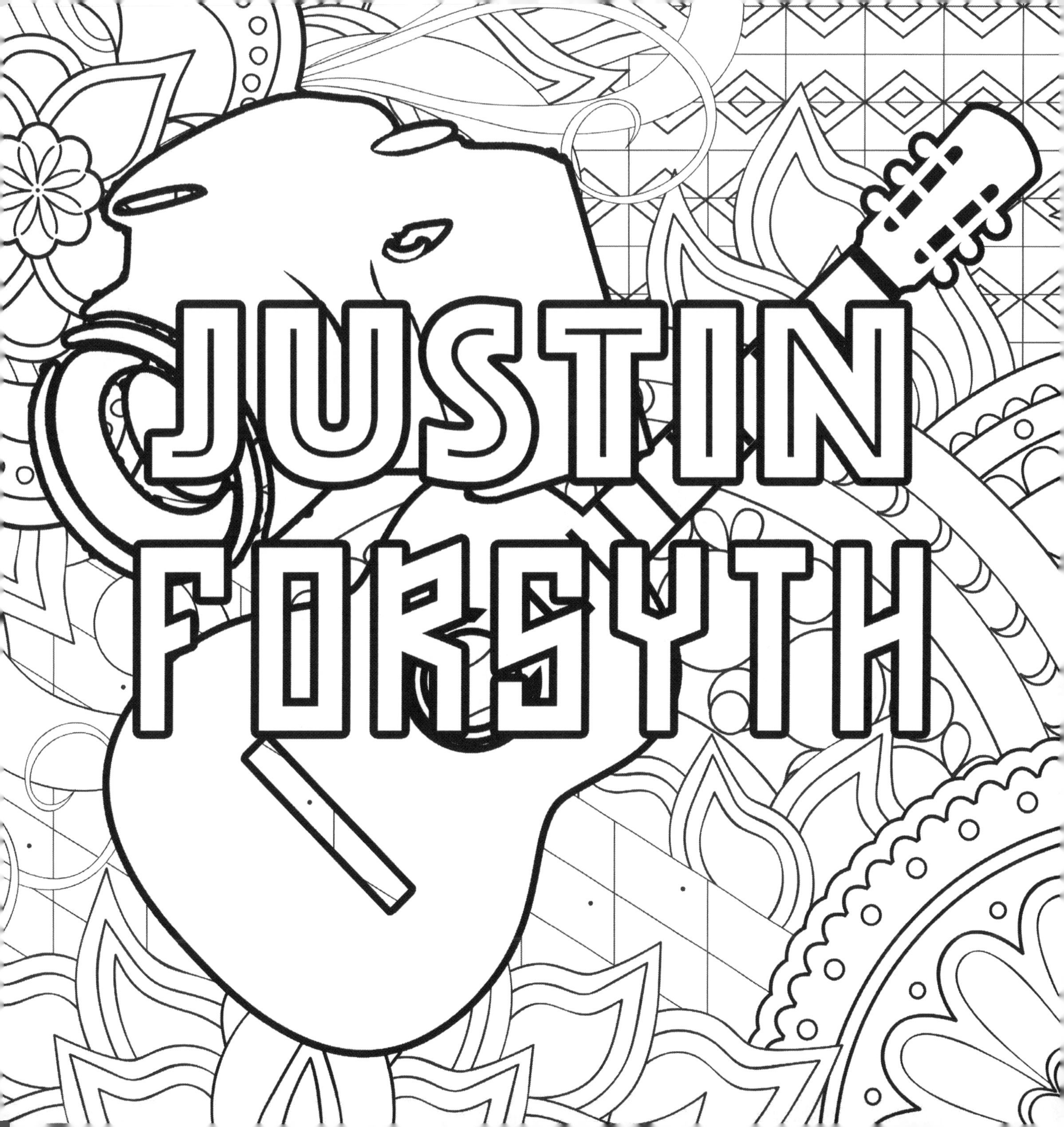
JUSTIN
FORSYTH

Kimberg

Bromberg

I RACE YOU.

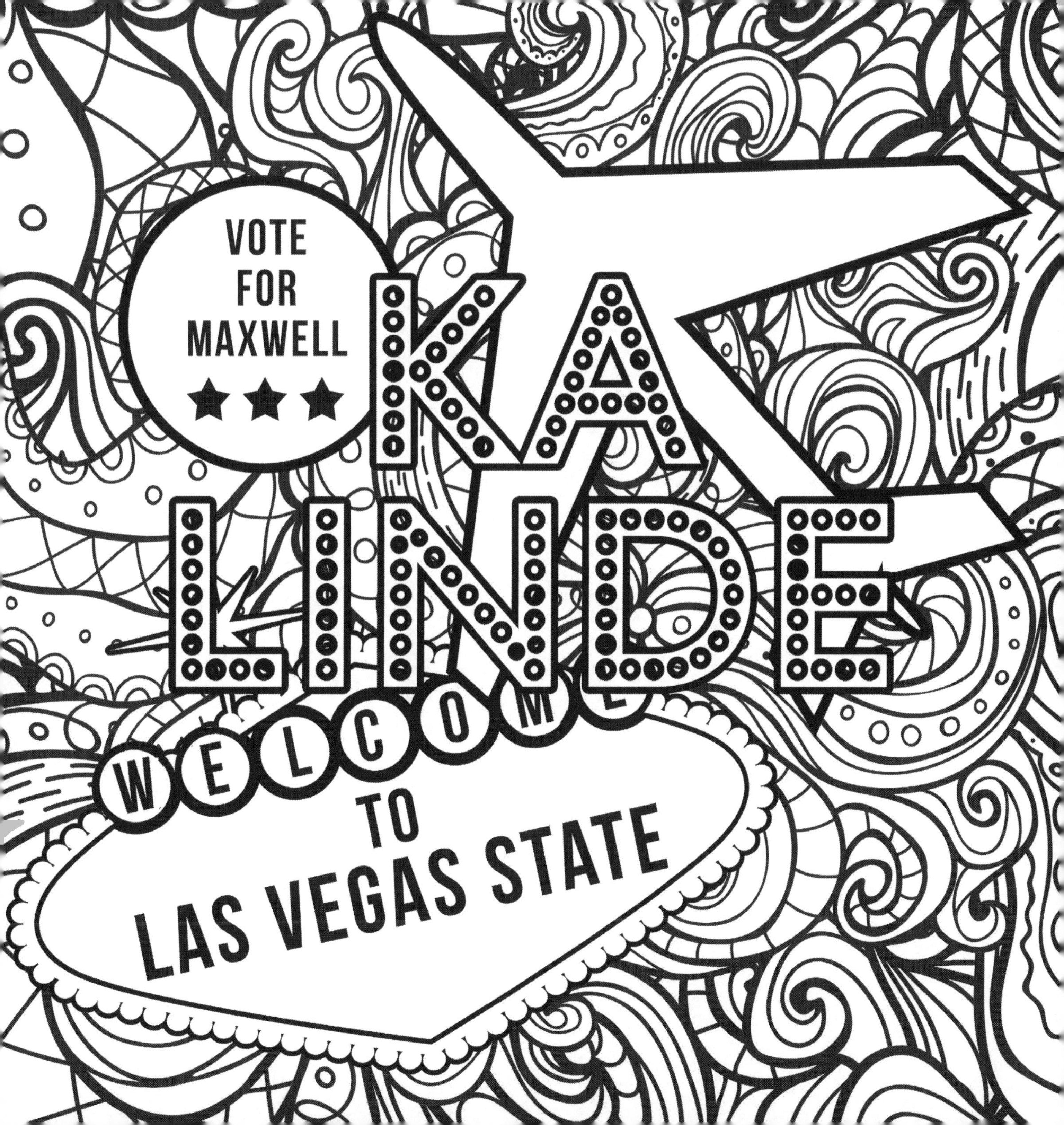
VOTE
FOR
MAXWELL
KA
LINDE
WELCOM
TO
LAS VEGAS STATE

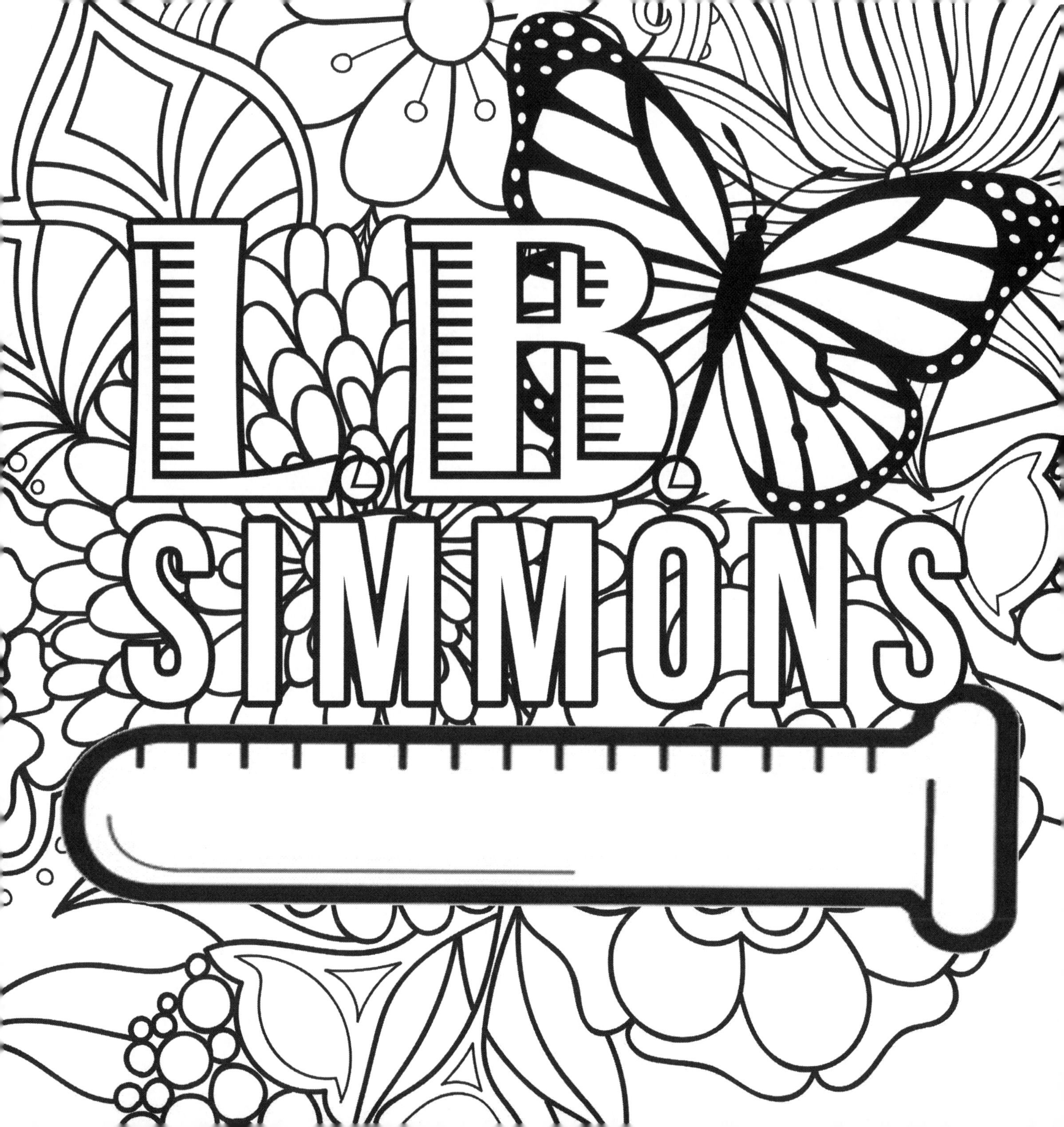
L.B.
SIMMONS

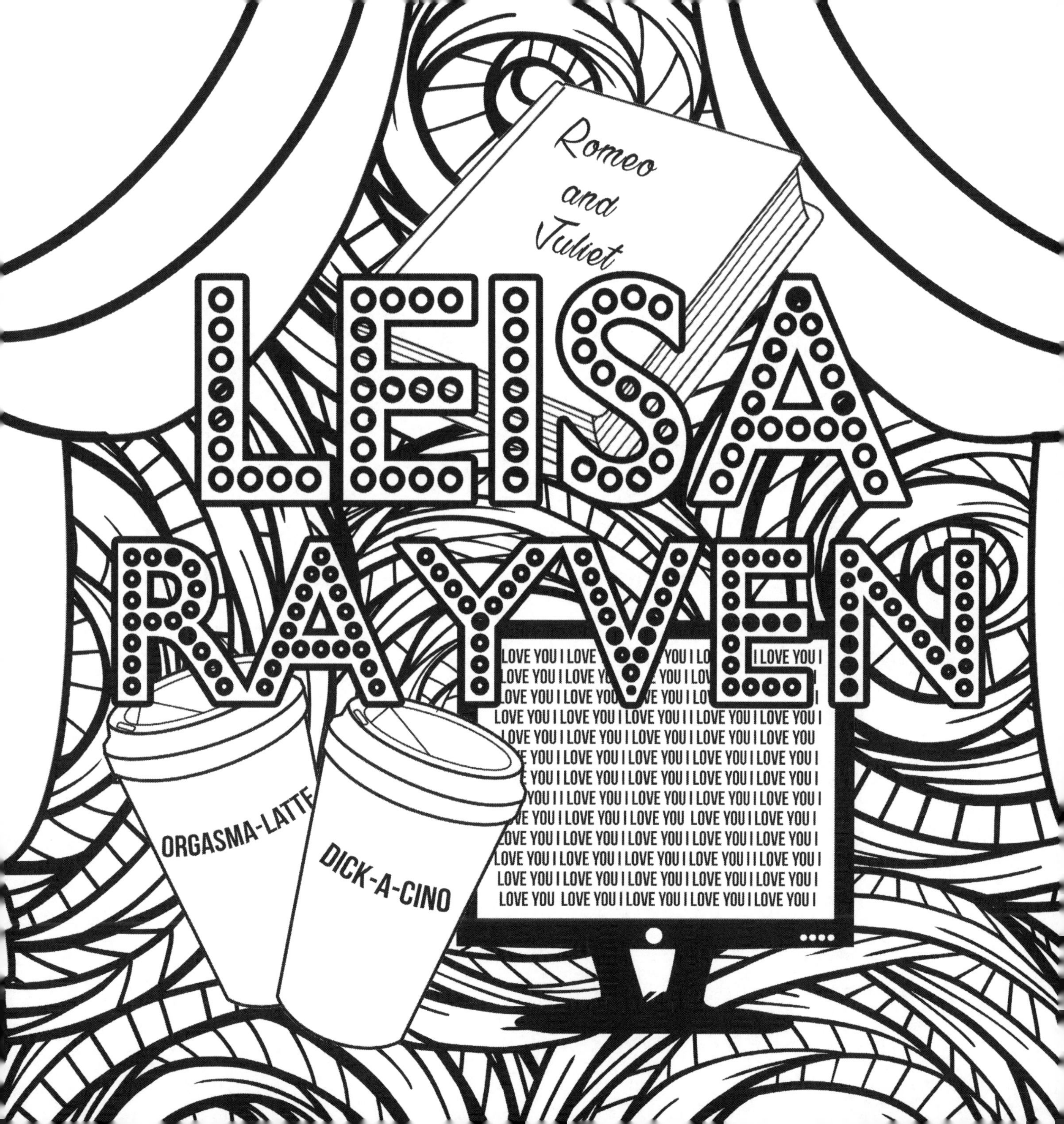
Romeo and Juliet
LEISA RAYVEN
ORGASMA-LATTE
DICK-A-CINO
LOVE YOU I LOVE YOU I LOVE YOU I LOVE YOU I LOVE YOU I
LOVE YOU I LOVE YOU I LOVE YOU I LOVE YOU I LOVE YOU
LOVE YOU I LOVE YOU I LOVE YOU I LOVE YOU I LOVE YOU I
LOVE YOU I LOVE YOU I LOVE YOU I LOVE YOU I LOVE YOU I
LOVE YOU I LOVE YOU I LOVE YOU I LOVE YOU I LOVE YOU I
LOVE YOU LOVE YOU I LOVE YOU I LOVE YOU I LOVE YOU I

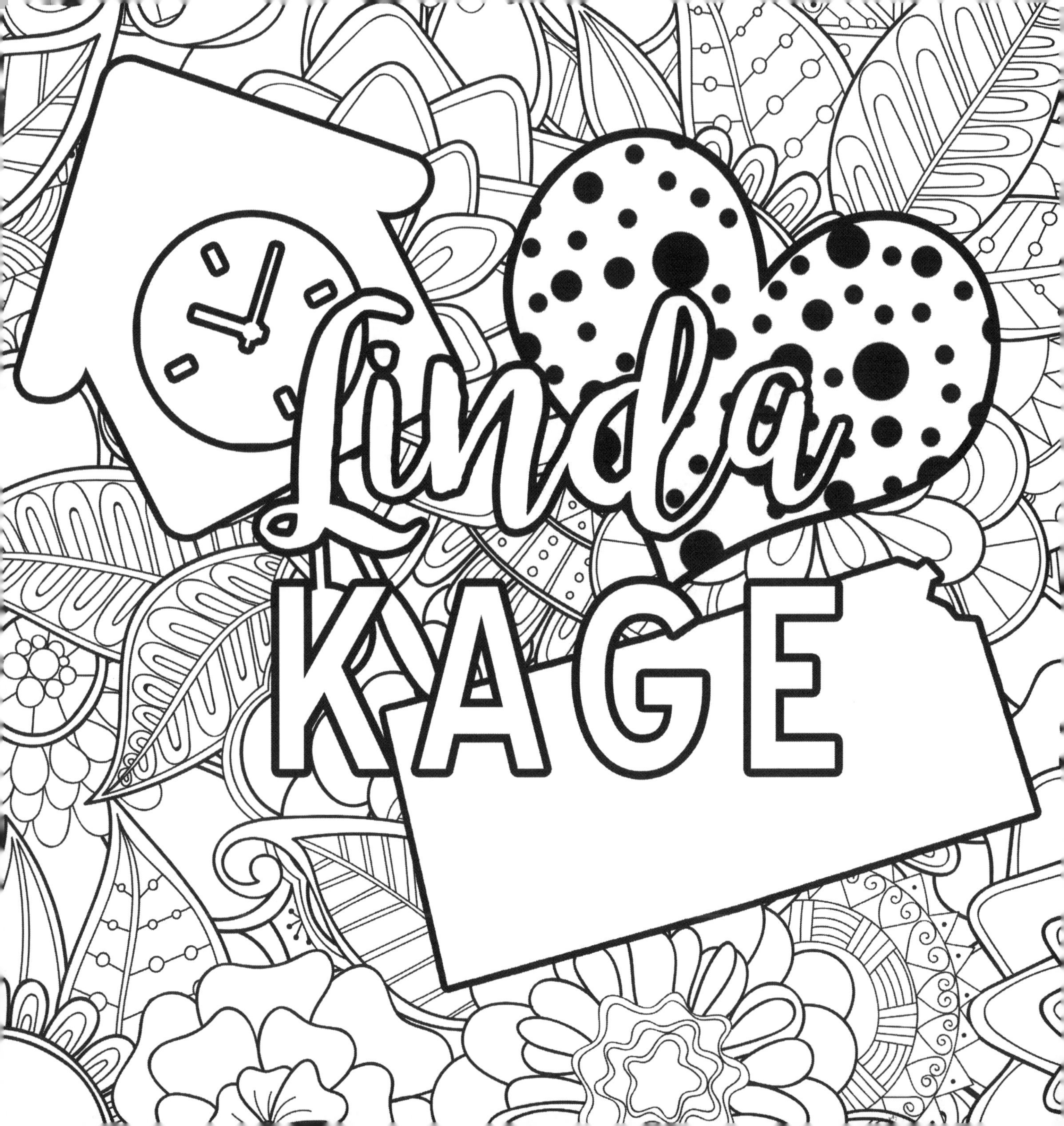
Linda
KAGE

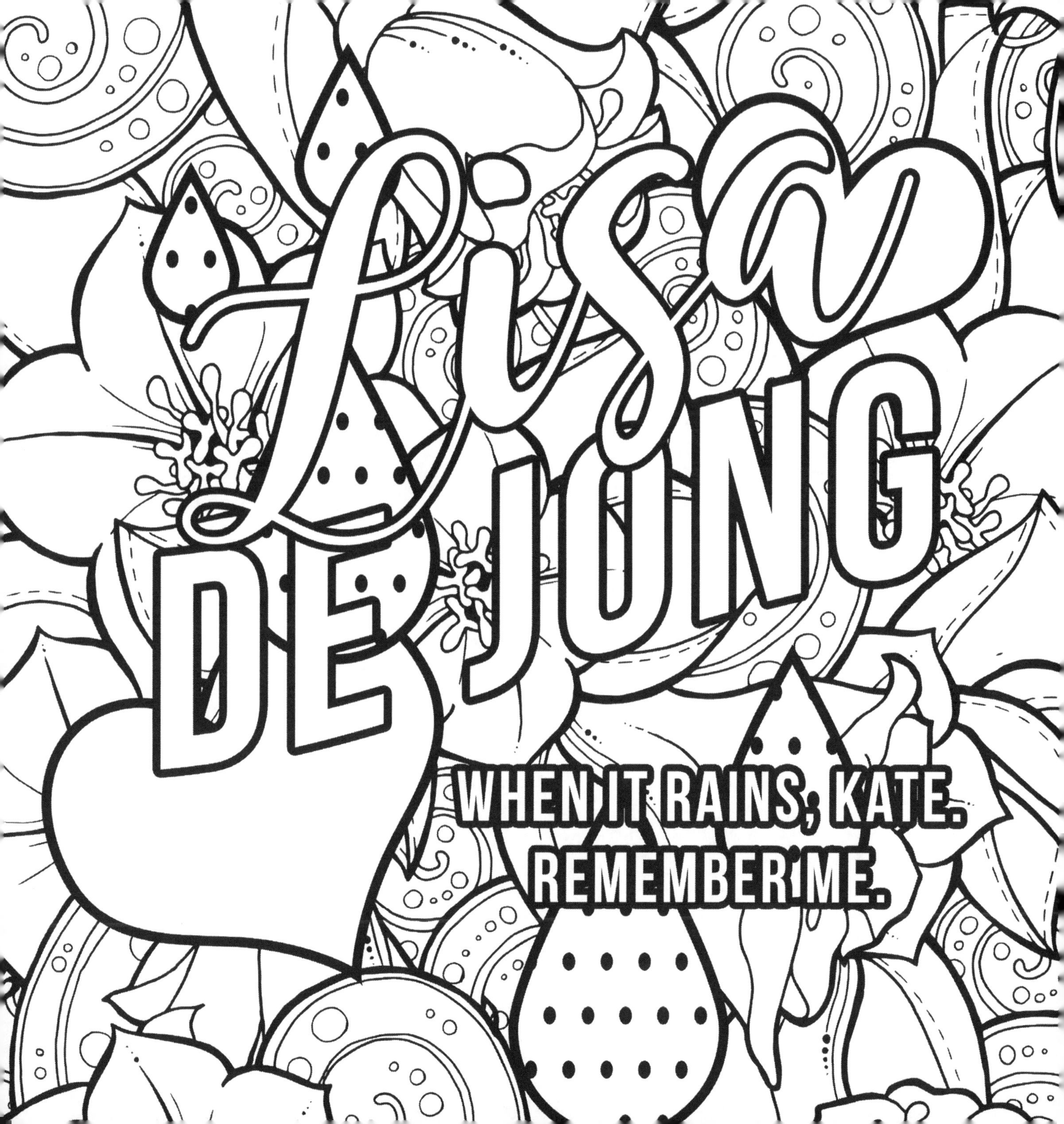
Lisa
DE JONG
WHEN IT RAINS, KATE.
REMEMBER ME.

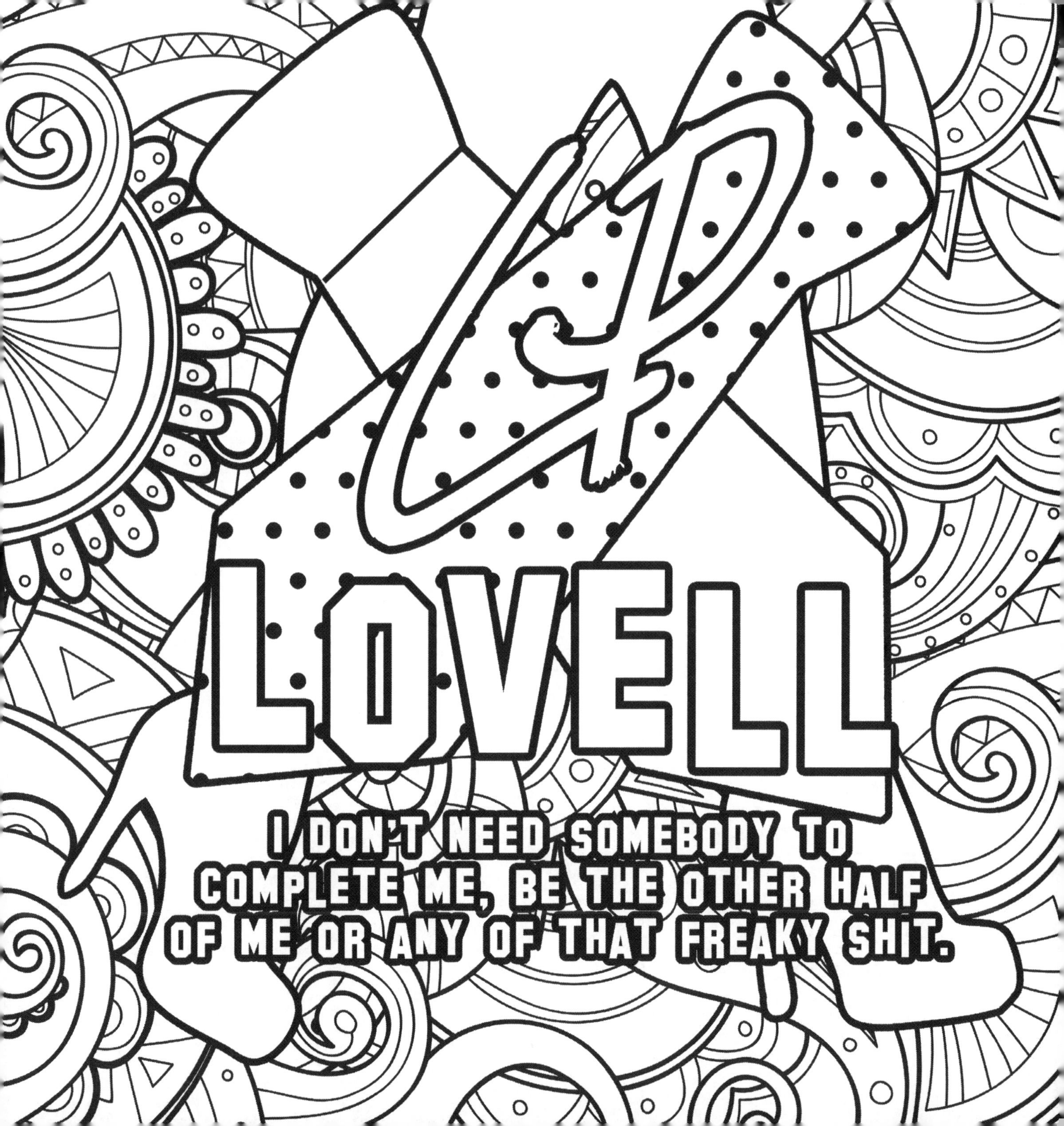
LOVELL
I DON'T NEED SOMEBODY TO COMPLETE ME, BE THE OTHER HALF OF ME OR ANY OF THAT FREAKY SHIT.

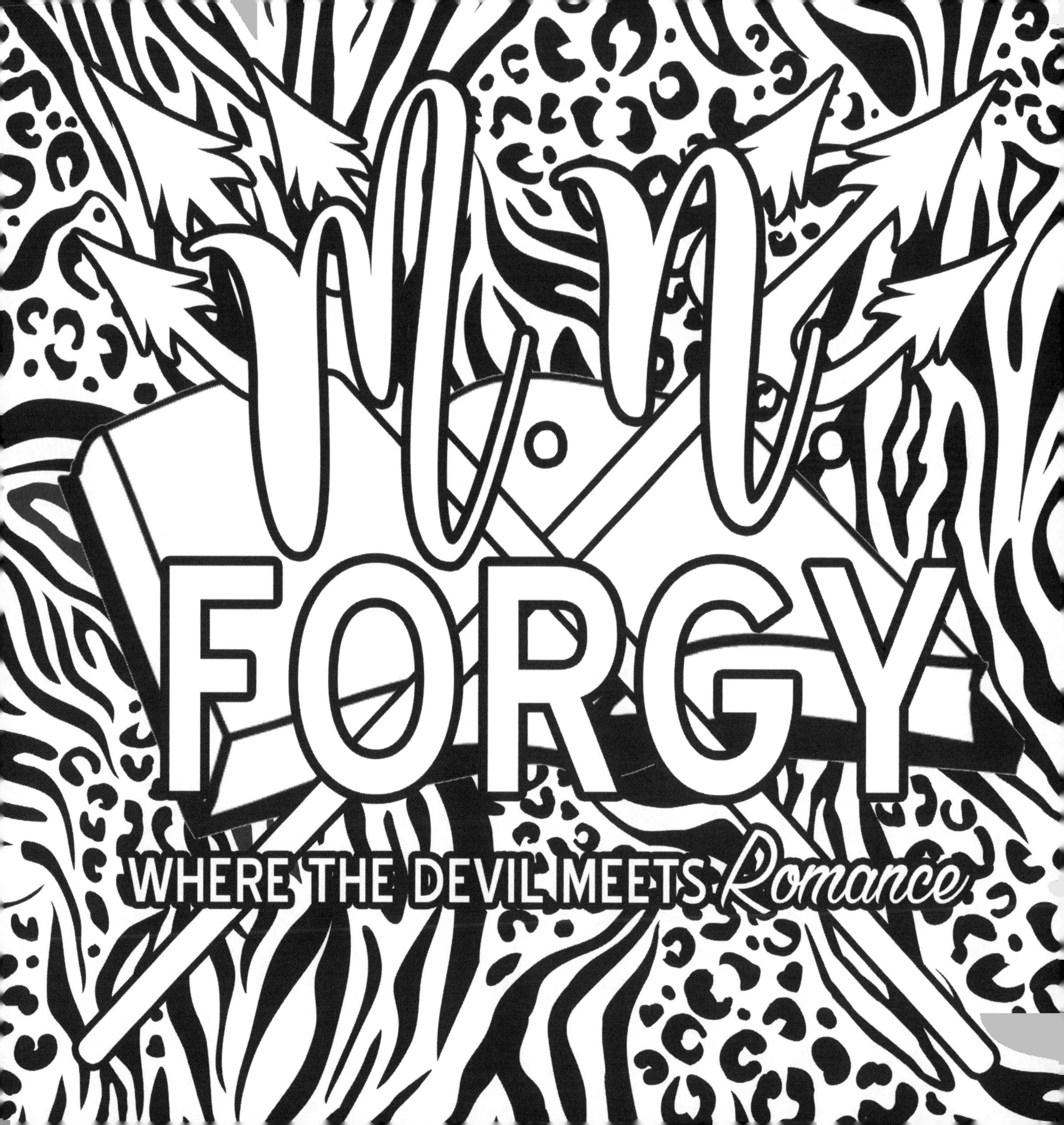
M.V.
FORGY
WHERE THE DEVIL MEETS Romance

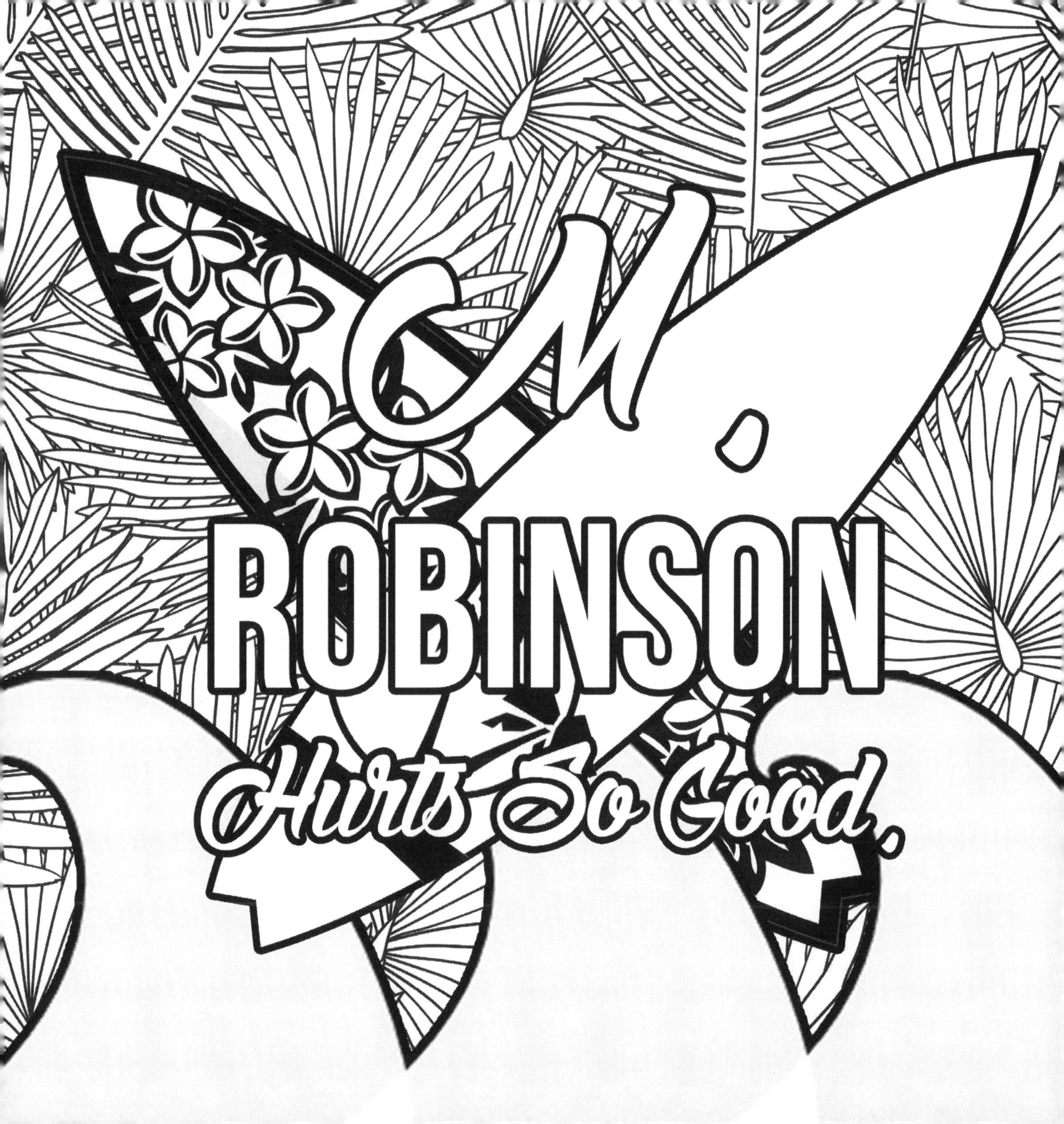
M.
ROBINSON
Hurts So Good.

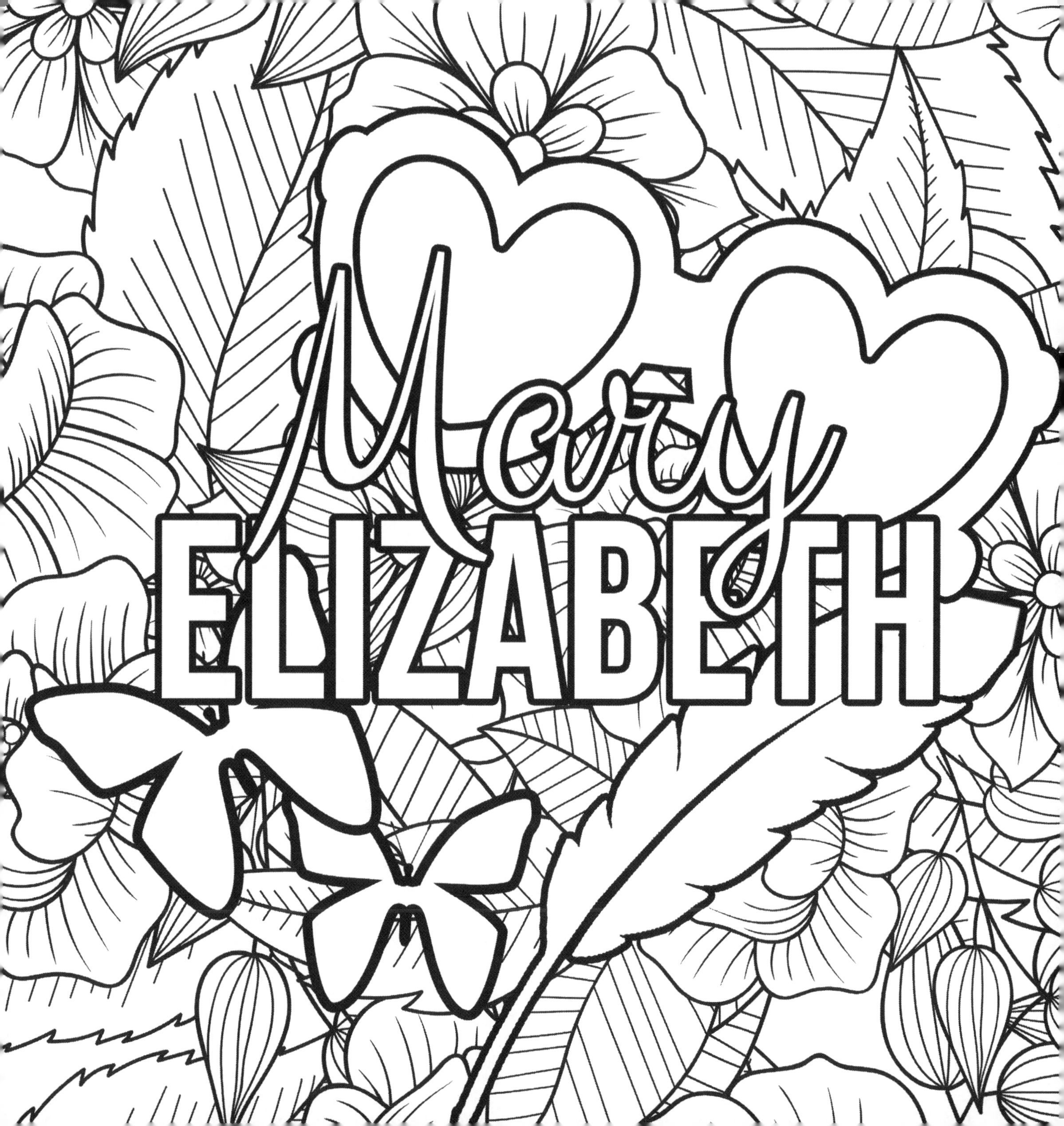
Mary
ELIZABETH

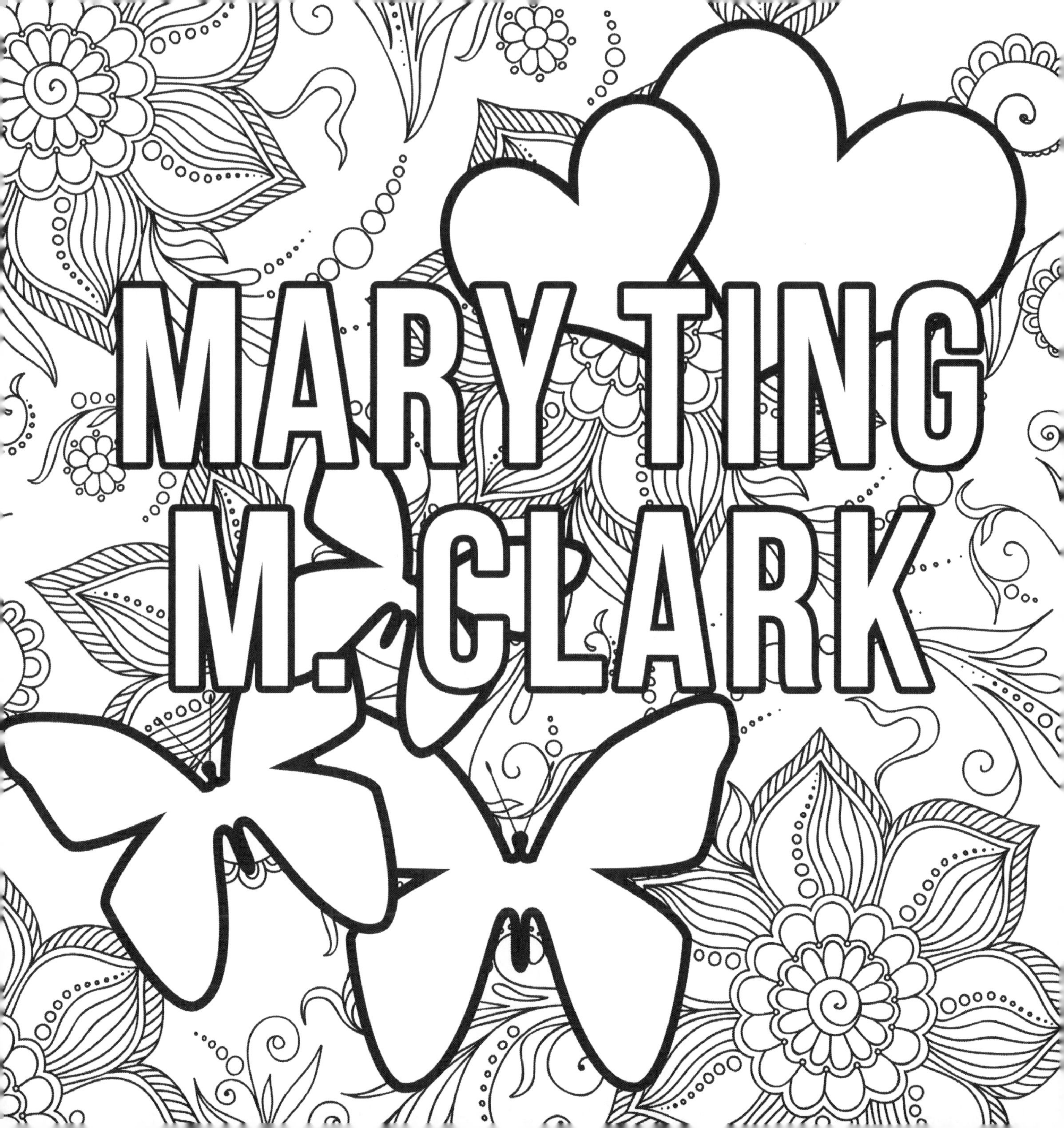
MARY TING
M. CLARK

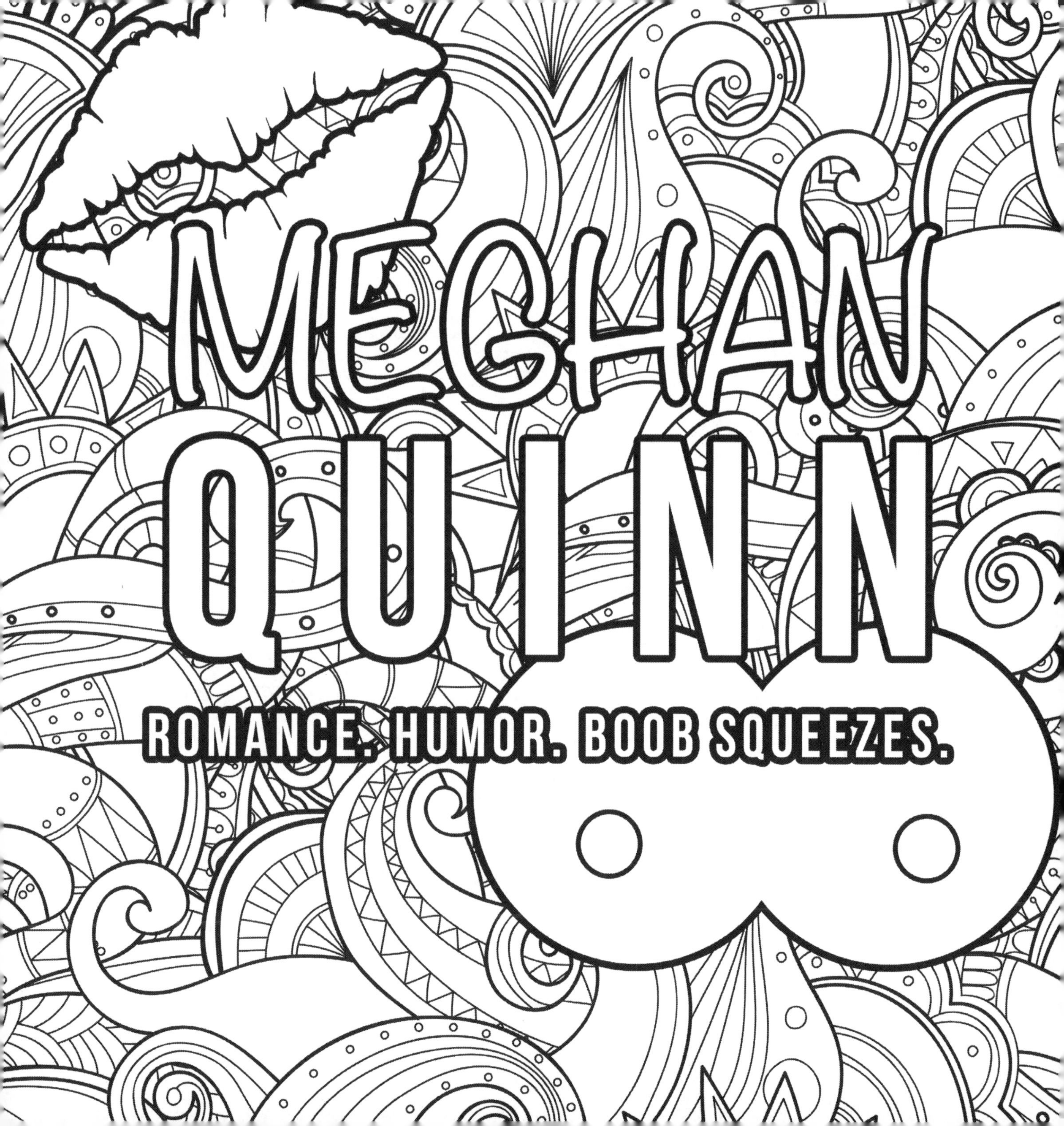
MEGHAN
QUINN
ROMANCE. HUMOR. BOOB SQUEEZES.

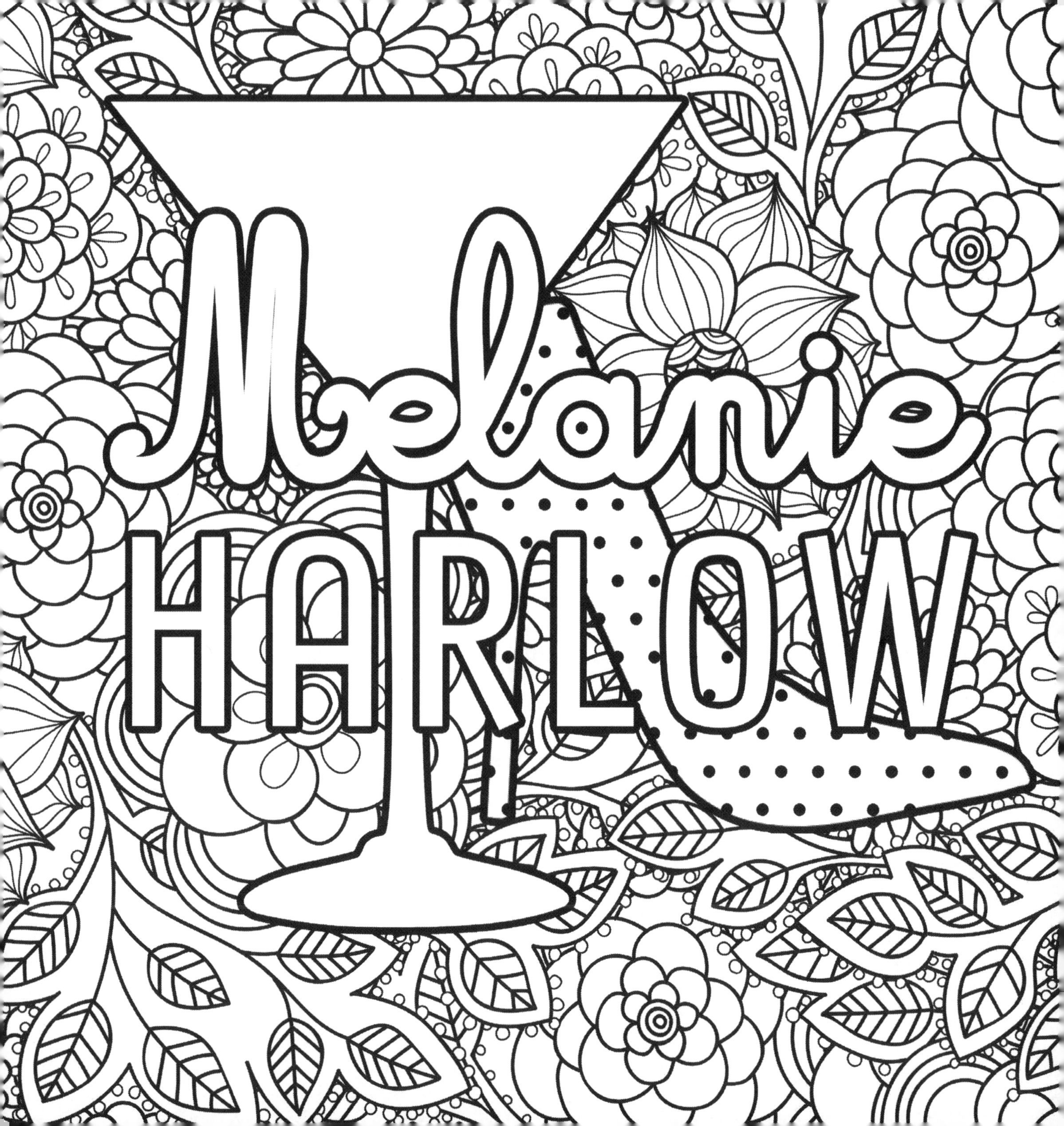
Melanie
HARLOW

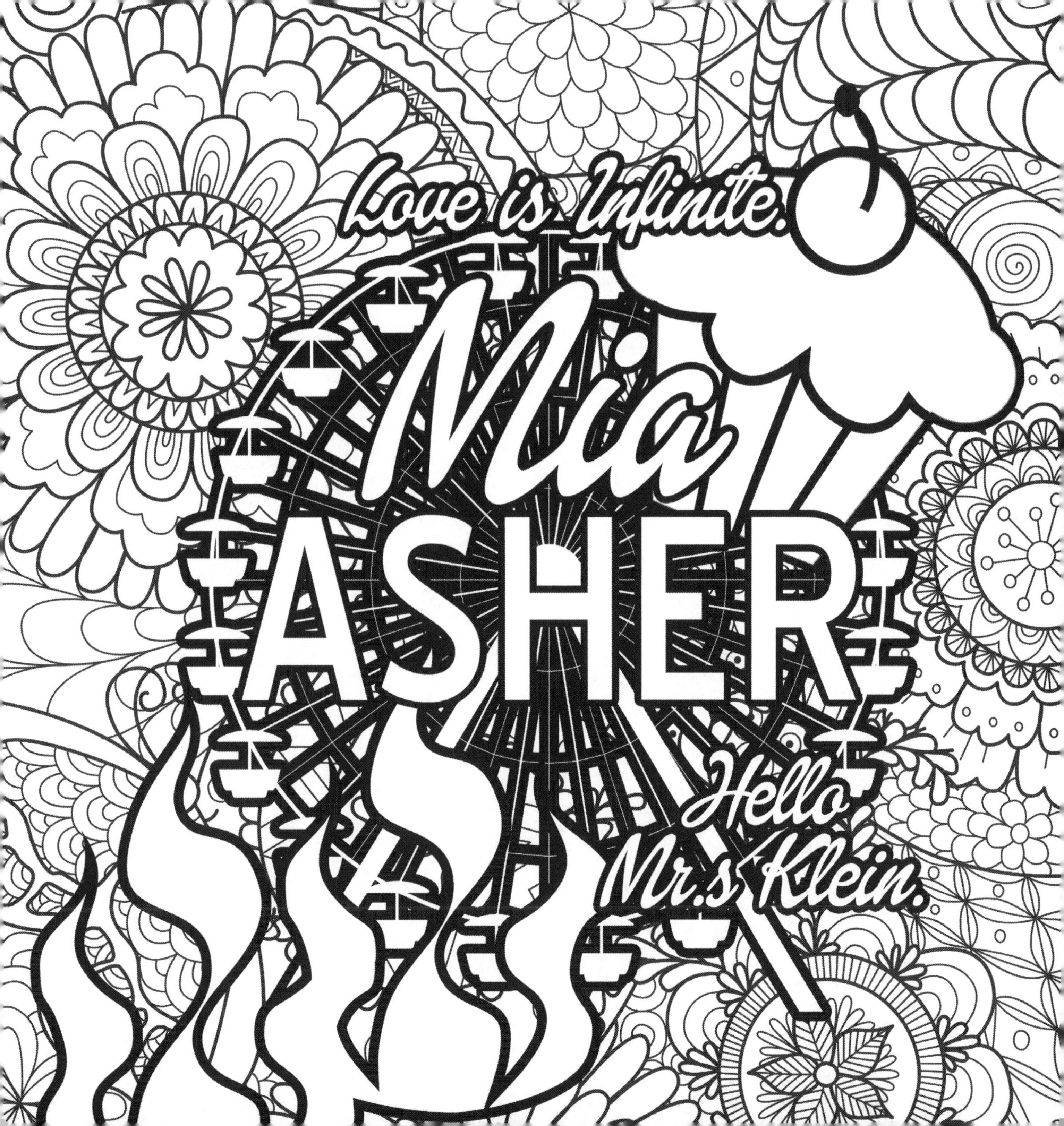
Love is Infinite.
Mia
ASHER
Hello
Mr.s Klein.

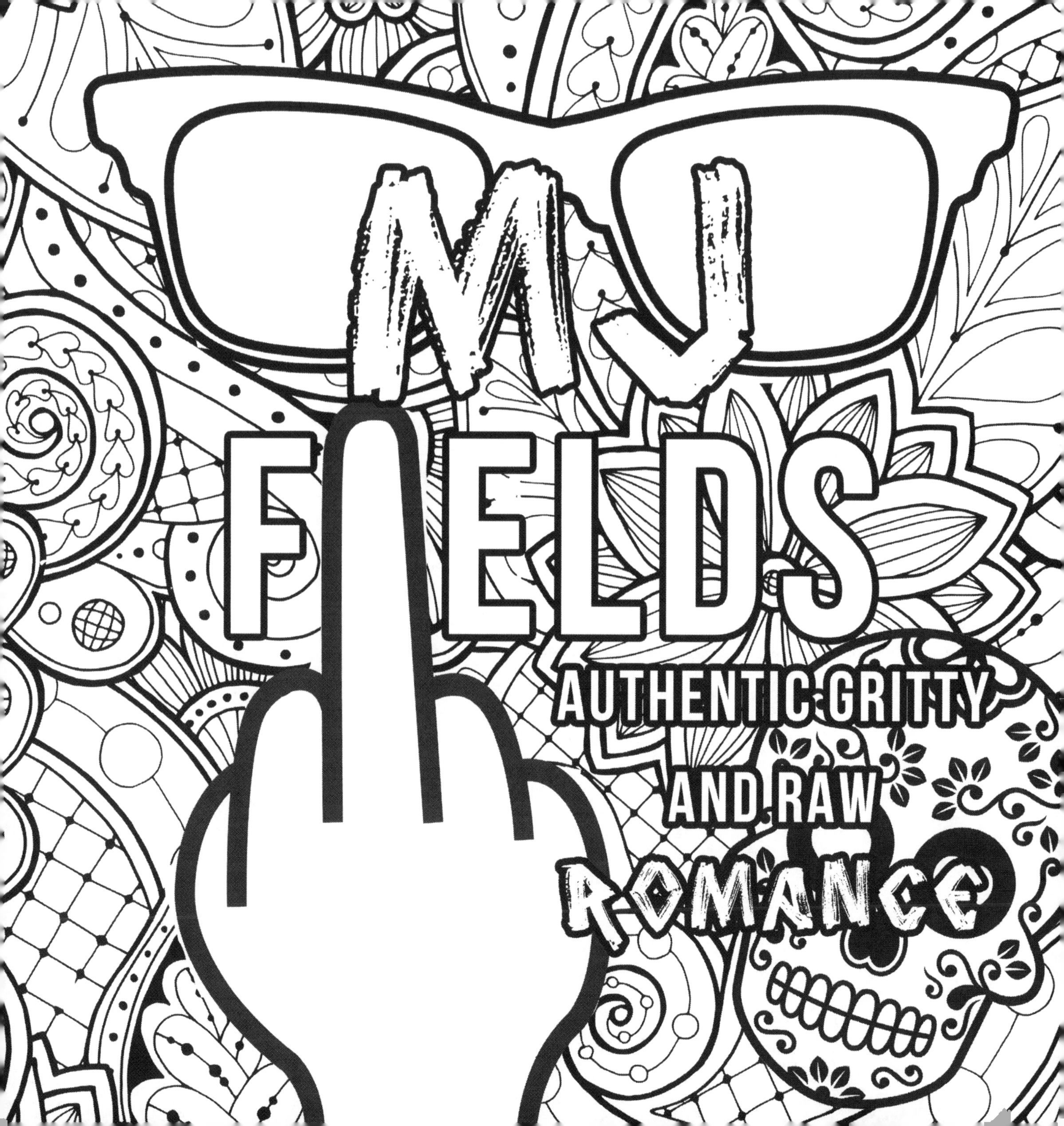
MY
FIELDS
AUTHENTIC GRITTY
AND RAW
ROMANCE

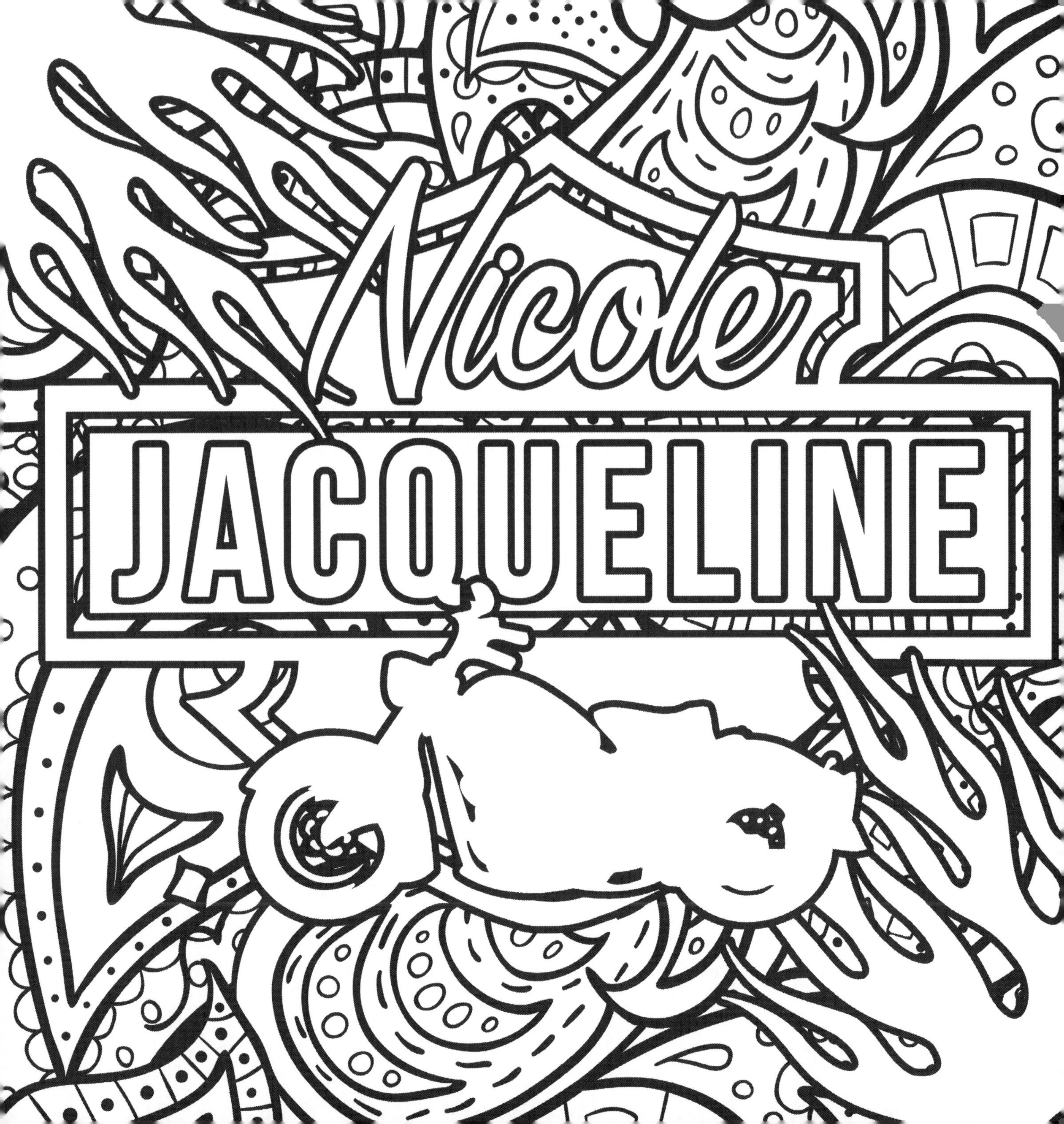
Nicole
JACQUELINE

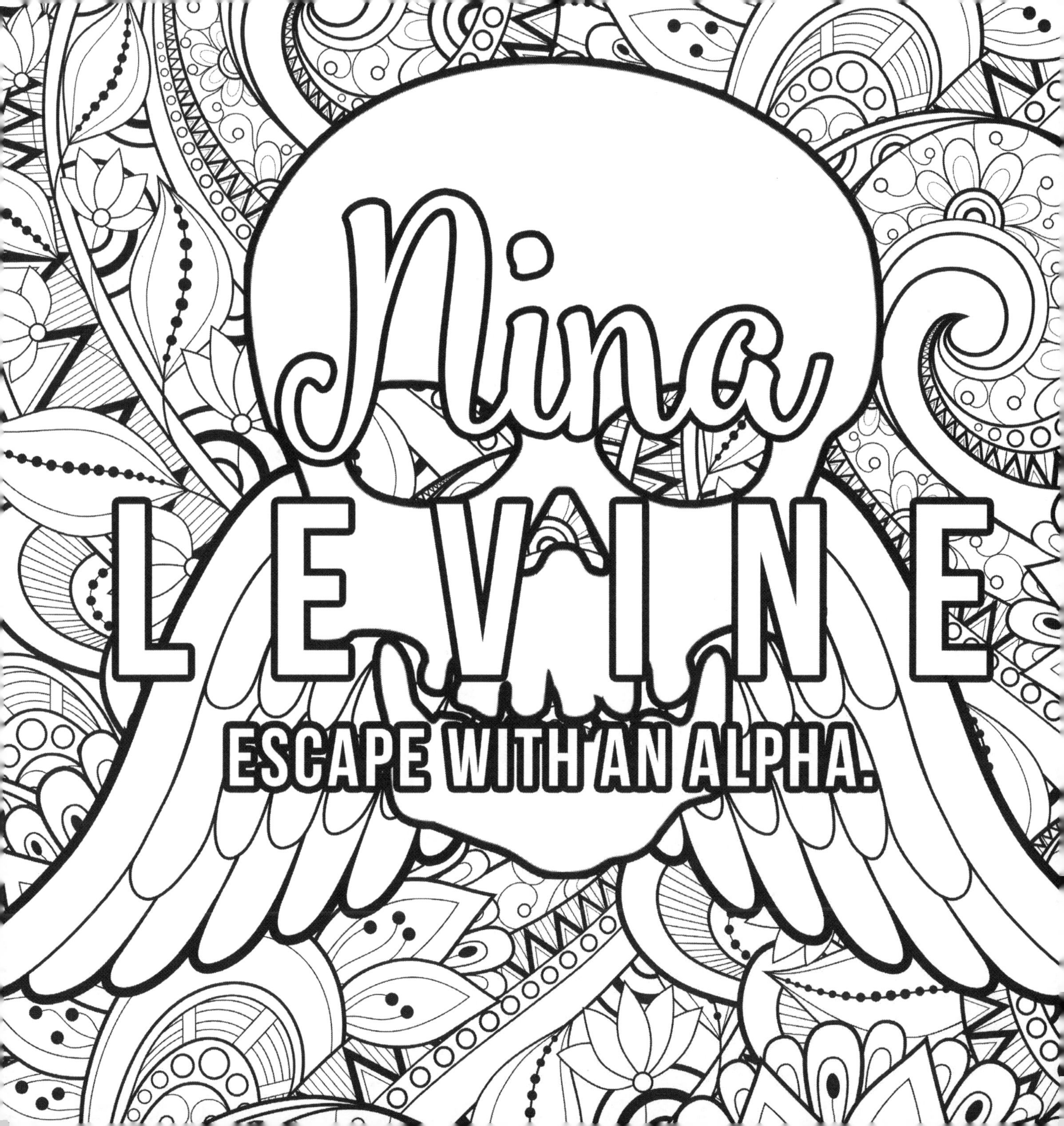
Nina
LEVINE
ESCAPE WITH AN ALPHA.

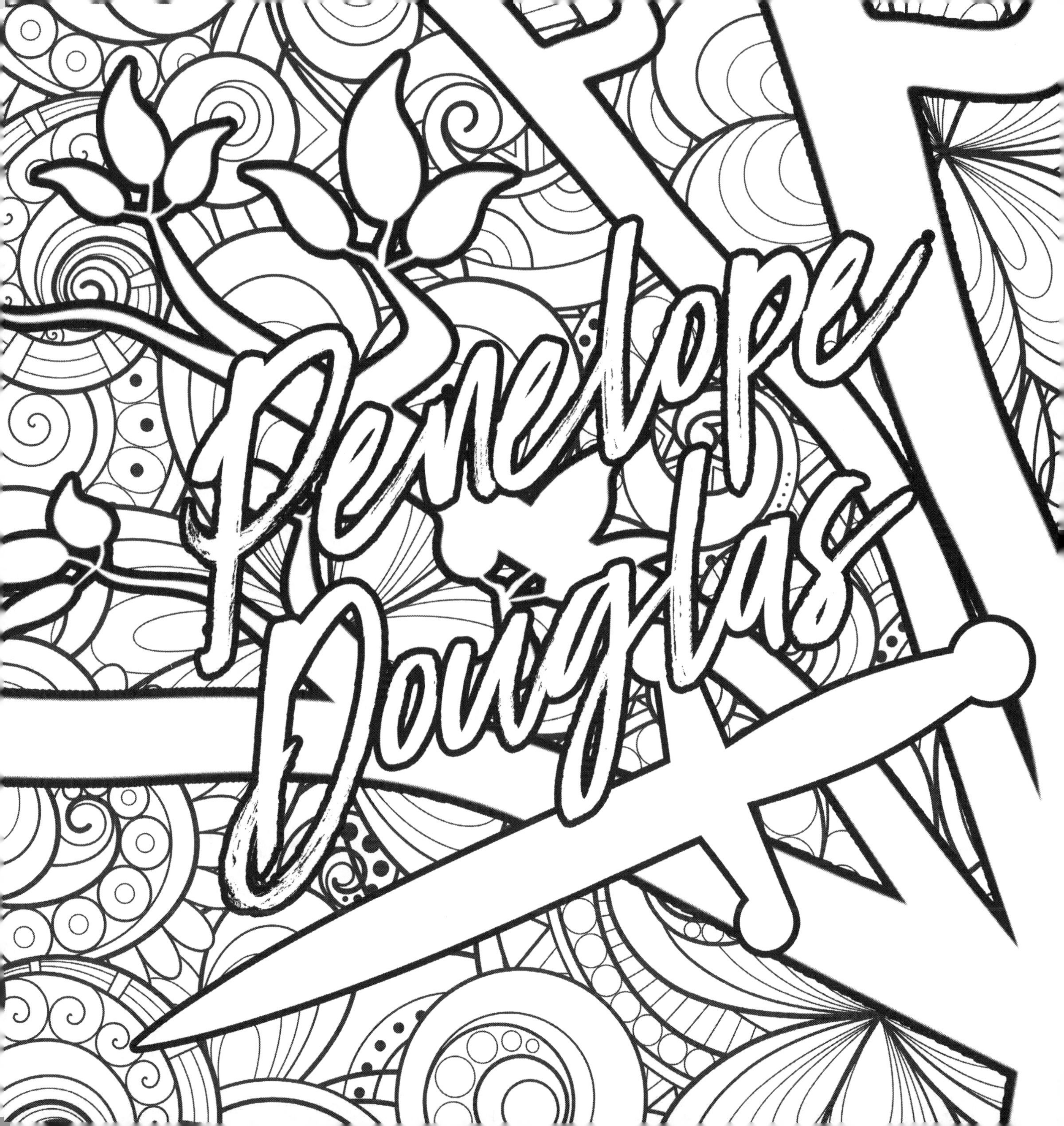
Penelope
Douglas

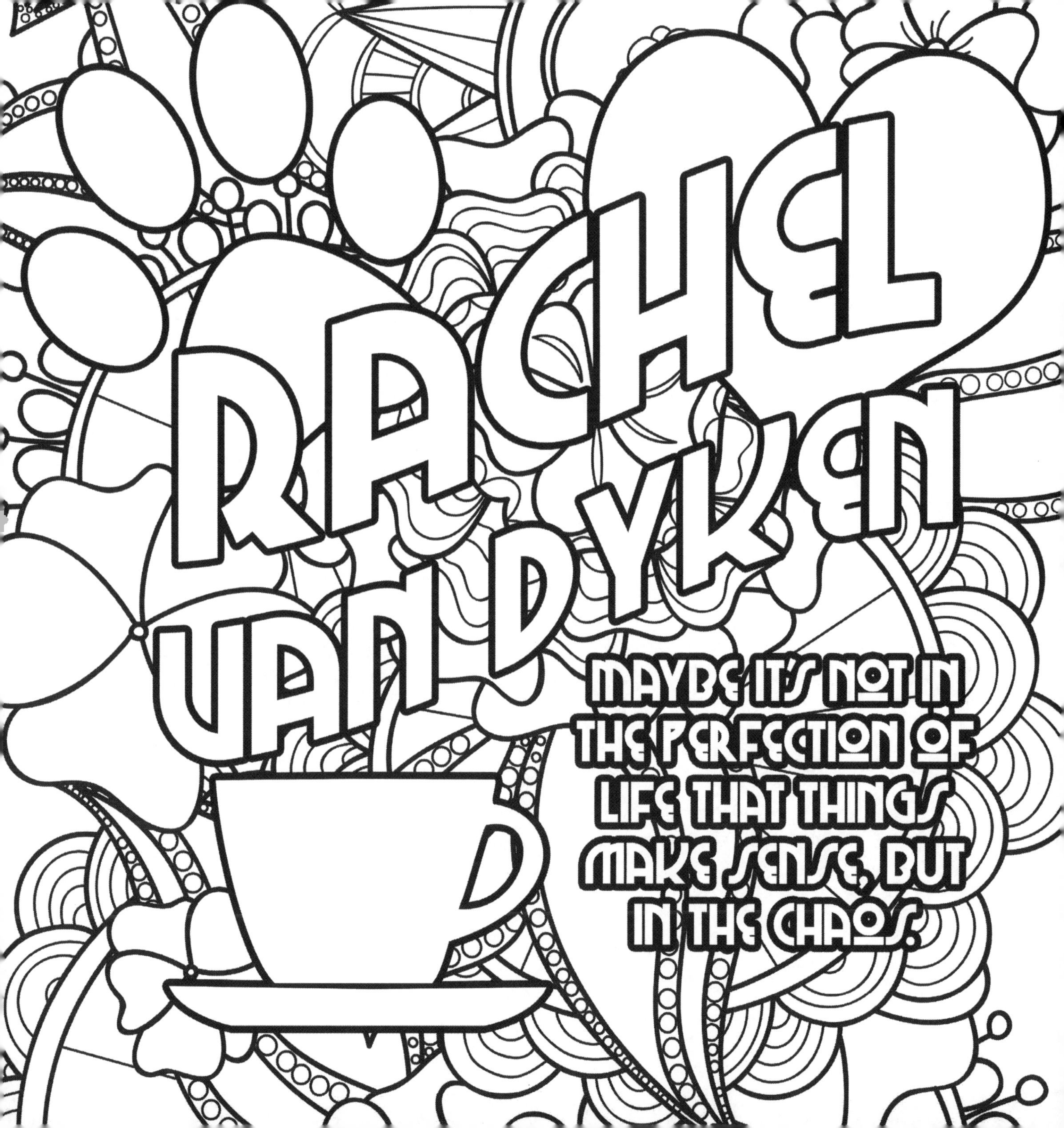
RACHEL VAN DYKEN
MAYBE IT'S NOT IN THE PERFECTION OF LIFE THAT THINGS MAKE SENSE, BUT IN THE CHAOS.

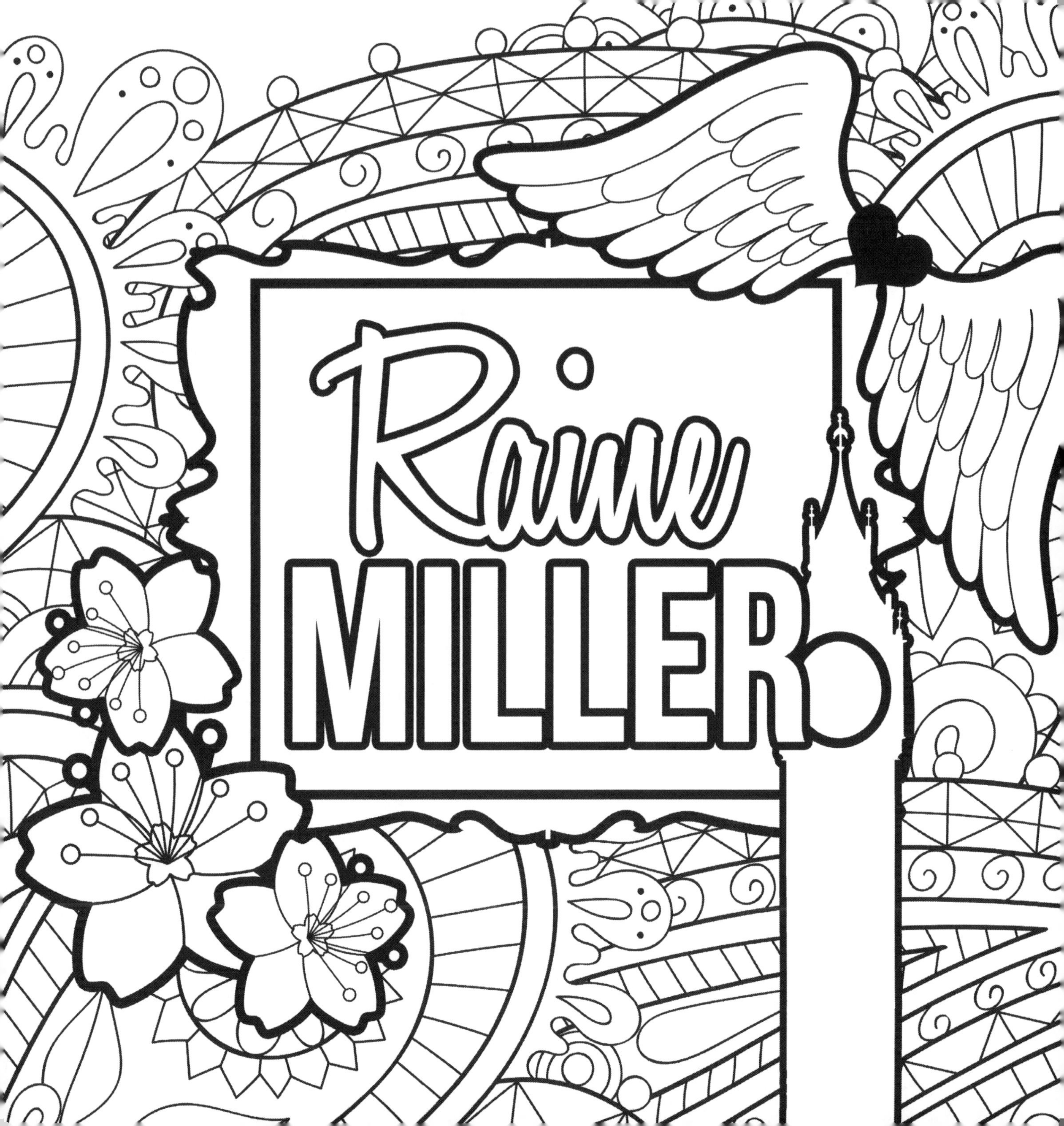
Raine
MILLER

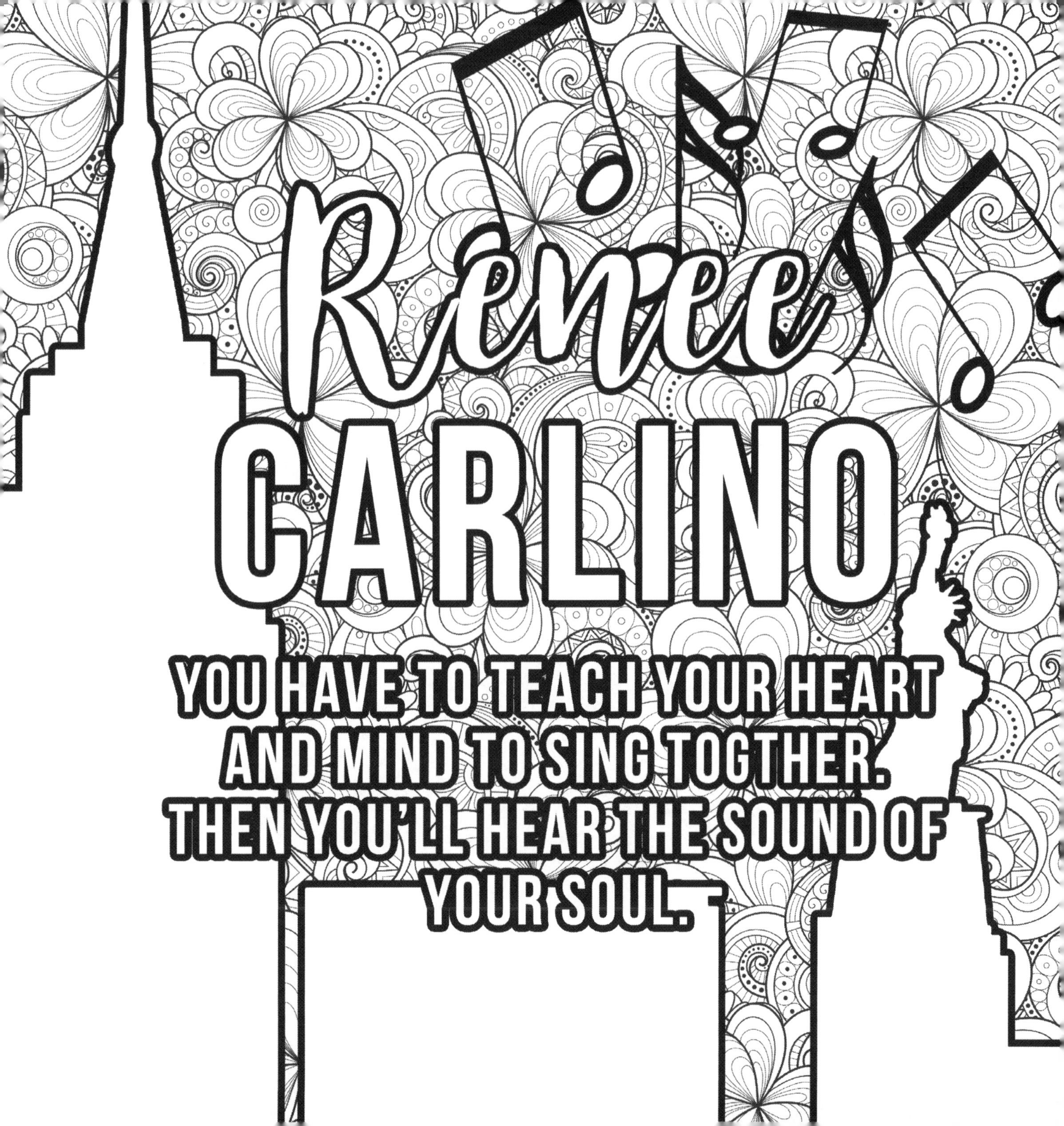
Renee
CARLINO
YOU HAVE TO TEACH YOUR HEART
AND MIND TO SING TOGTHER.
THEN YOU'LL HEAR THE SOUND OF
YOUR SOUL.

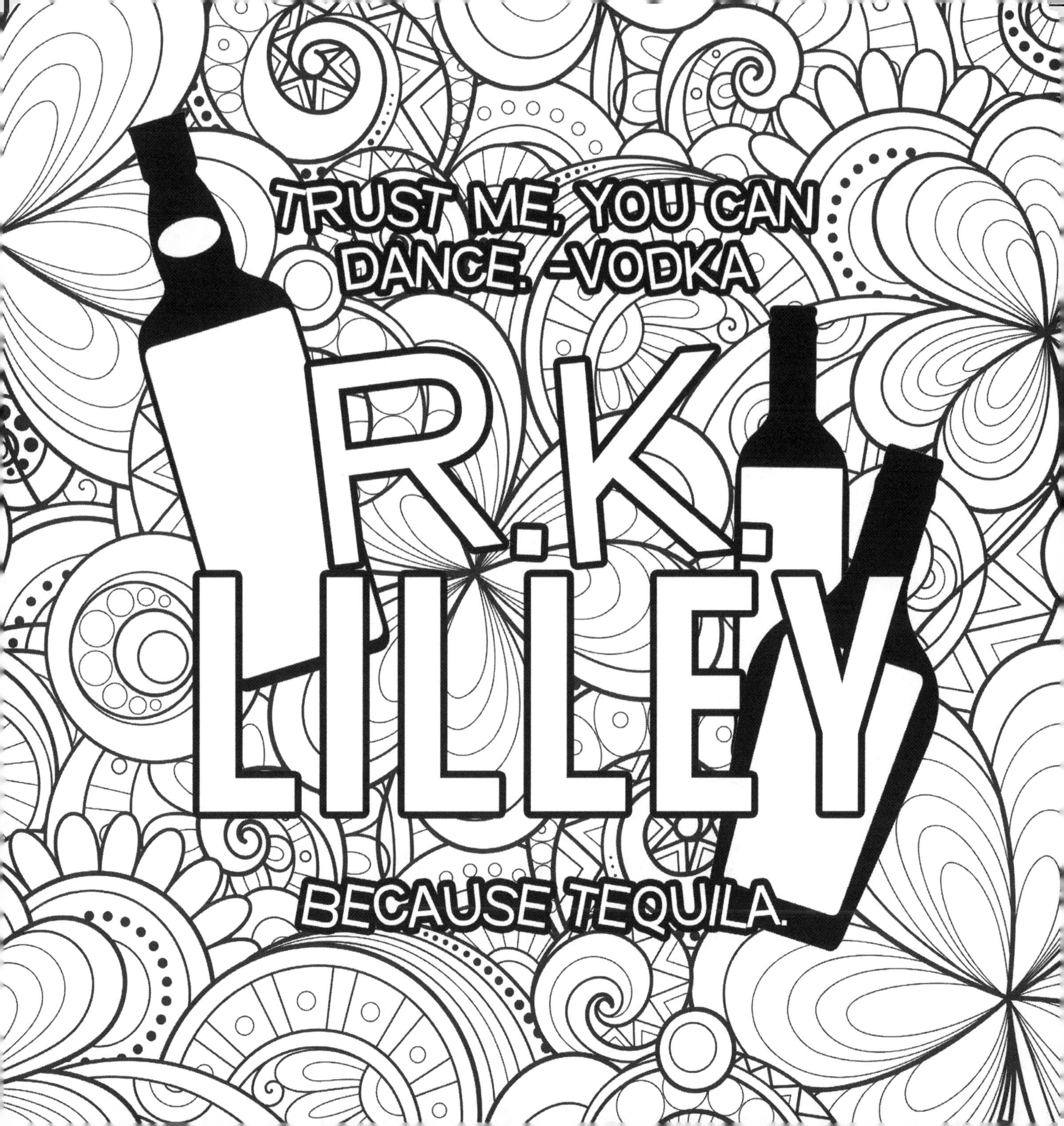
TRUST ME, YOU CAN DANCE. -VODKA
R.K. LILLEY
BECAUSE TEQUILA.

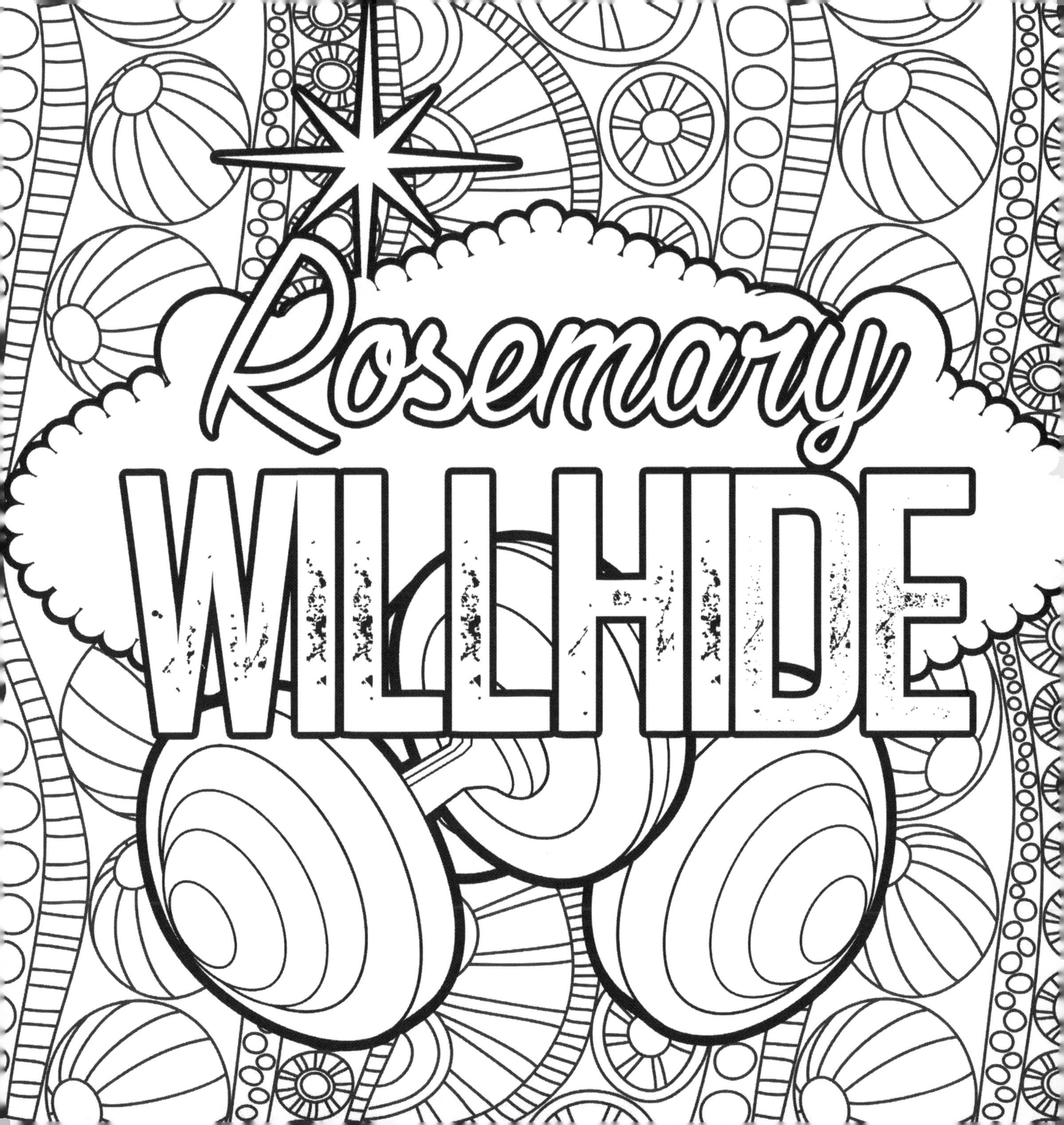
Rosemary
WILLHIDE

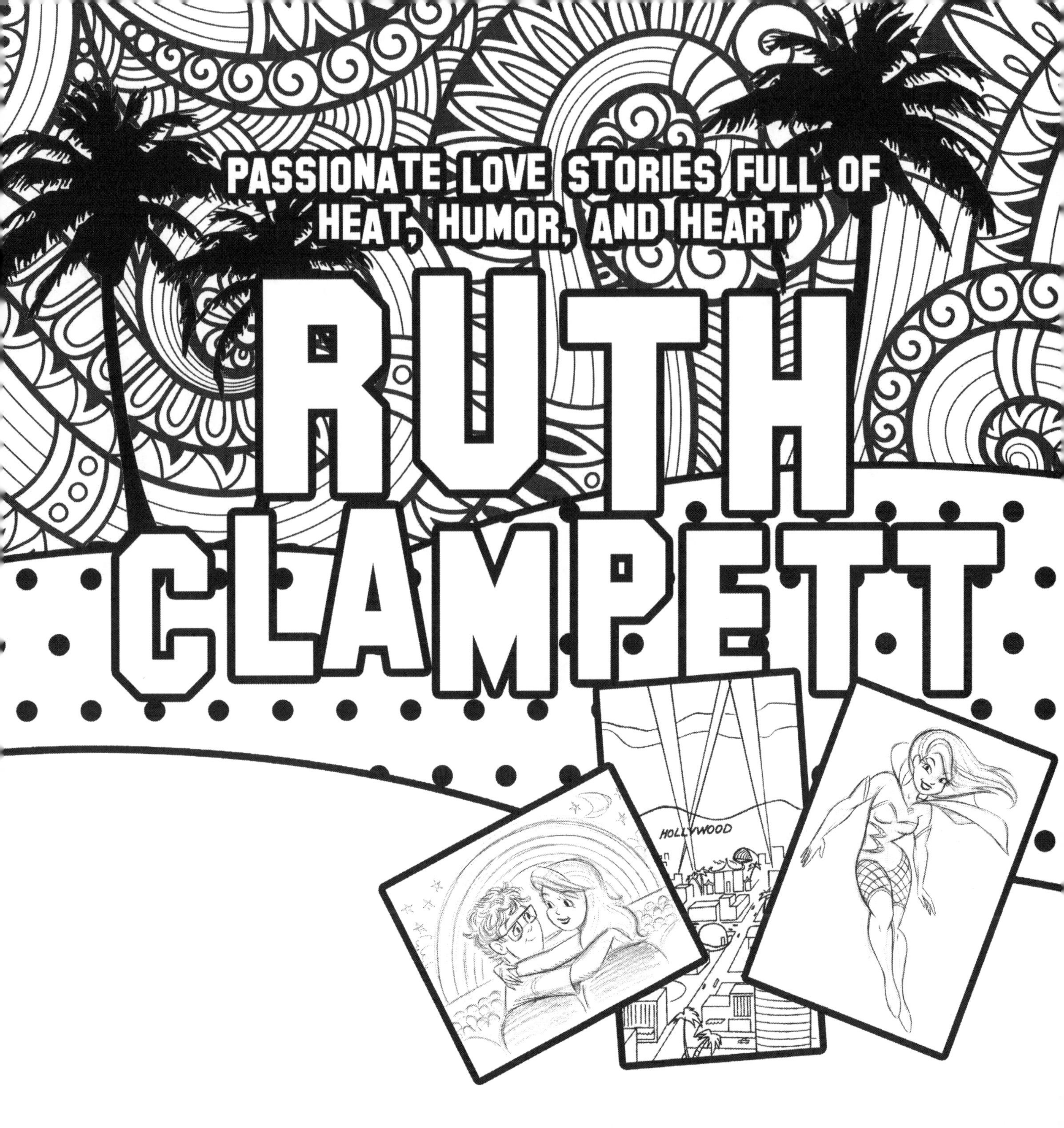
PASSIONATE LOVE STORIES FULL OF
HEAT, HUMOR, AND HEART
RUTH
CLAMPETT
HOLLYWOOD

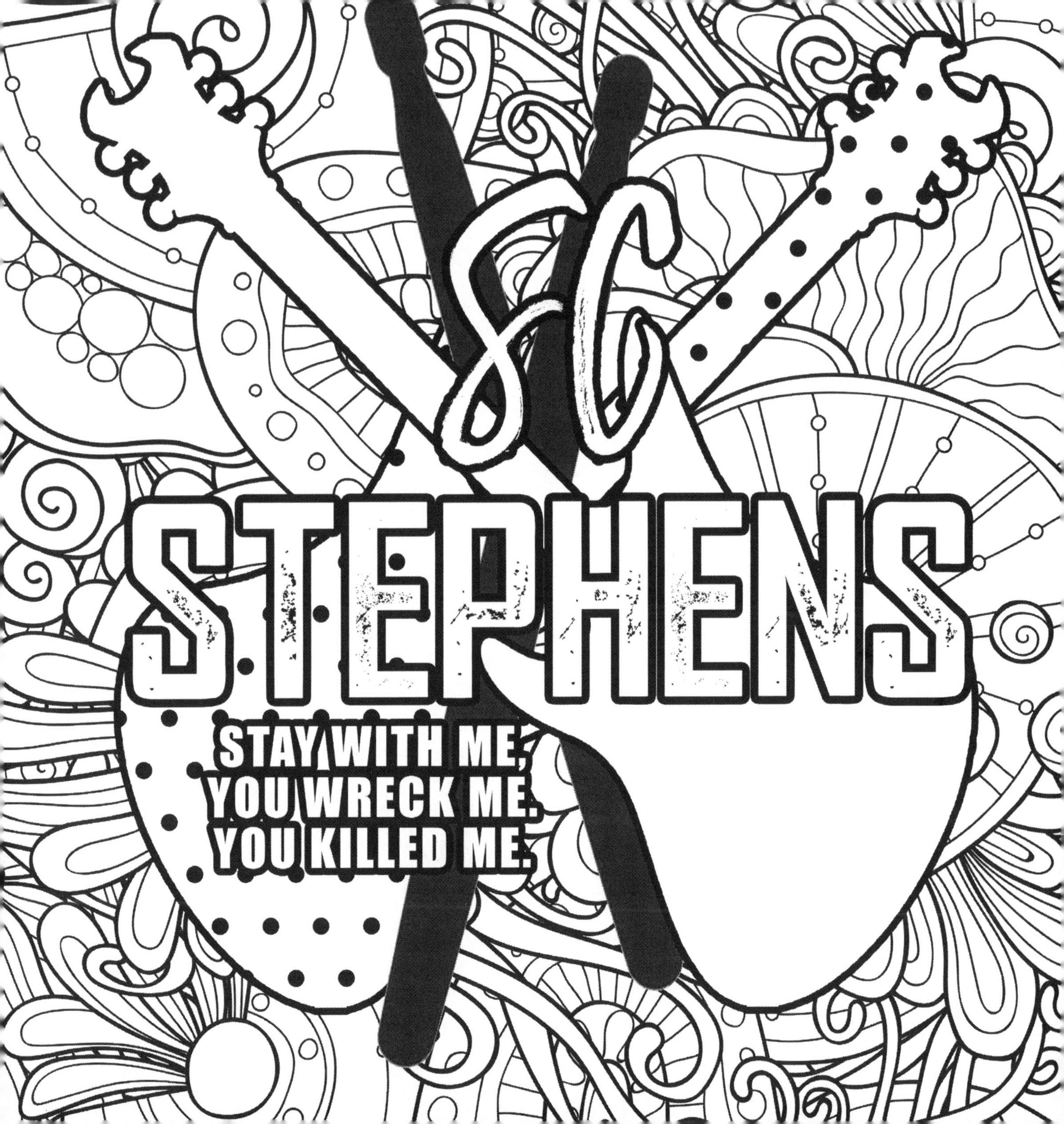
SC
STEPHENS
STAY WITH ME,
YOU WRECK ME.
YOU KILLED ME.

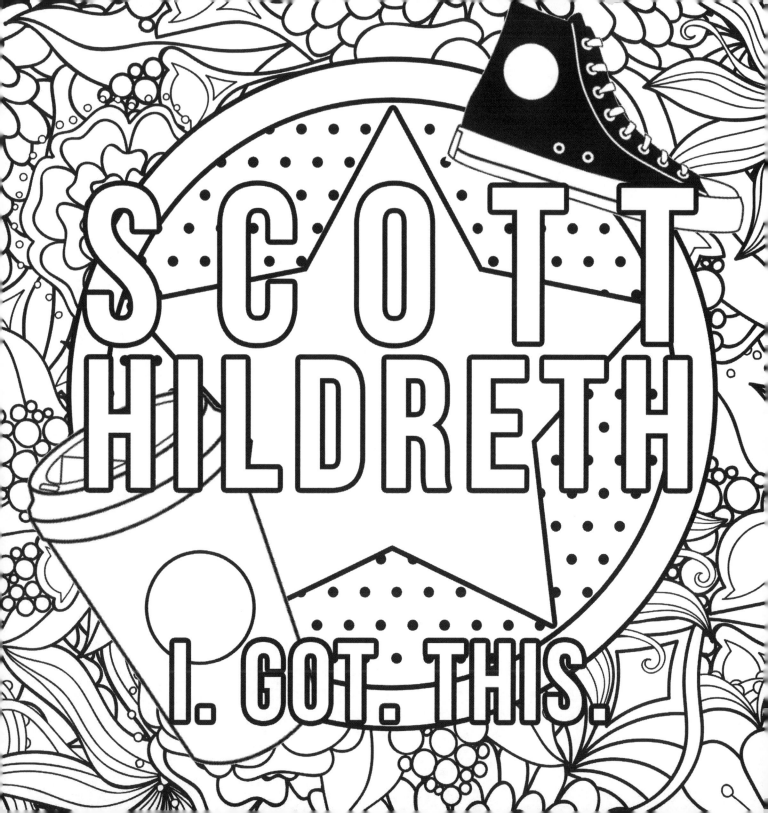

SCOTT HILDRETH

I. GOT. THIS.

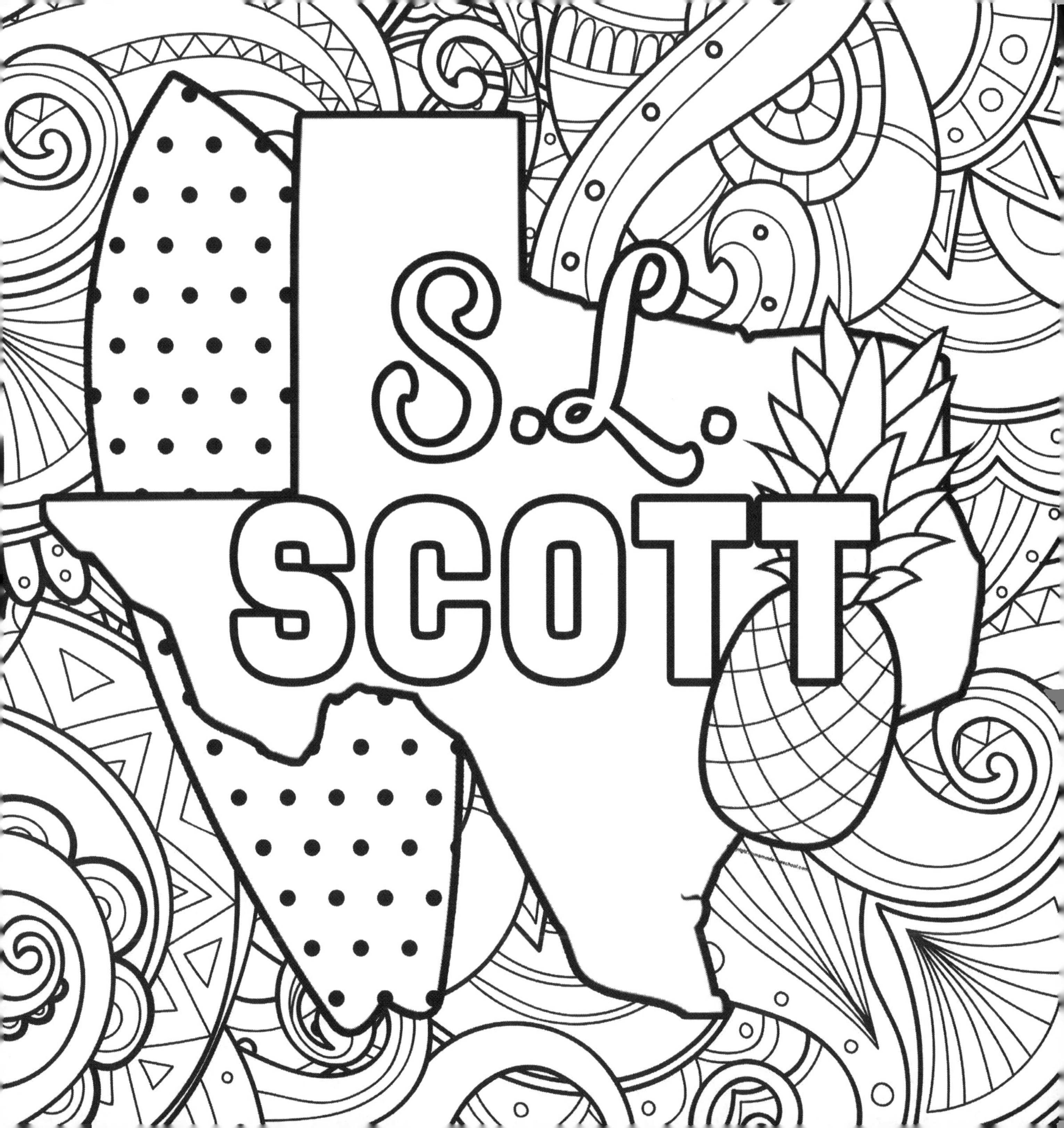
S.L.
SCOTT

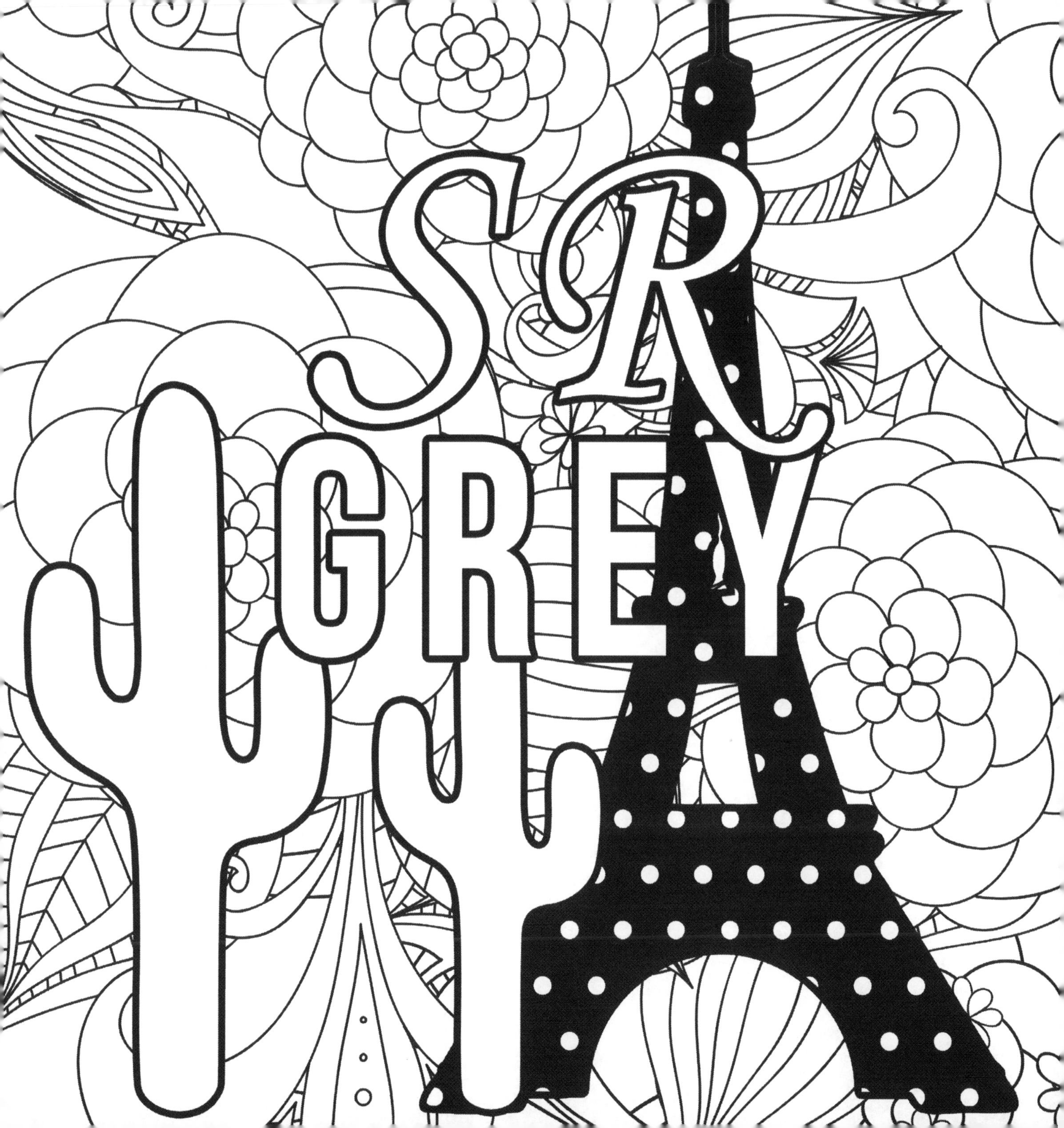
SR
GREY

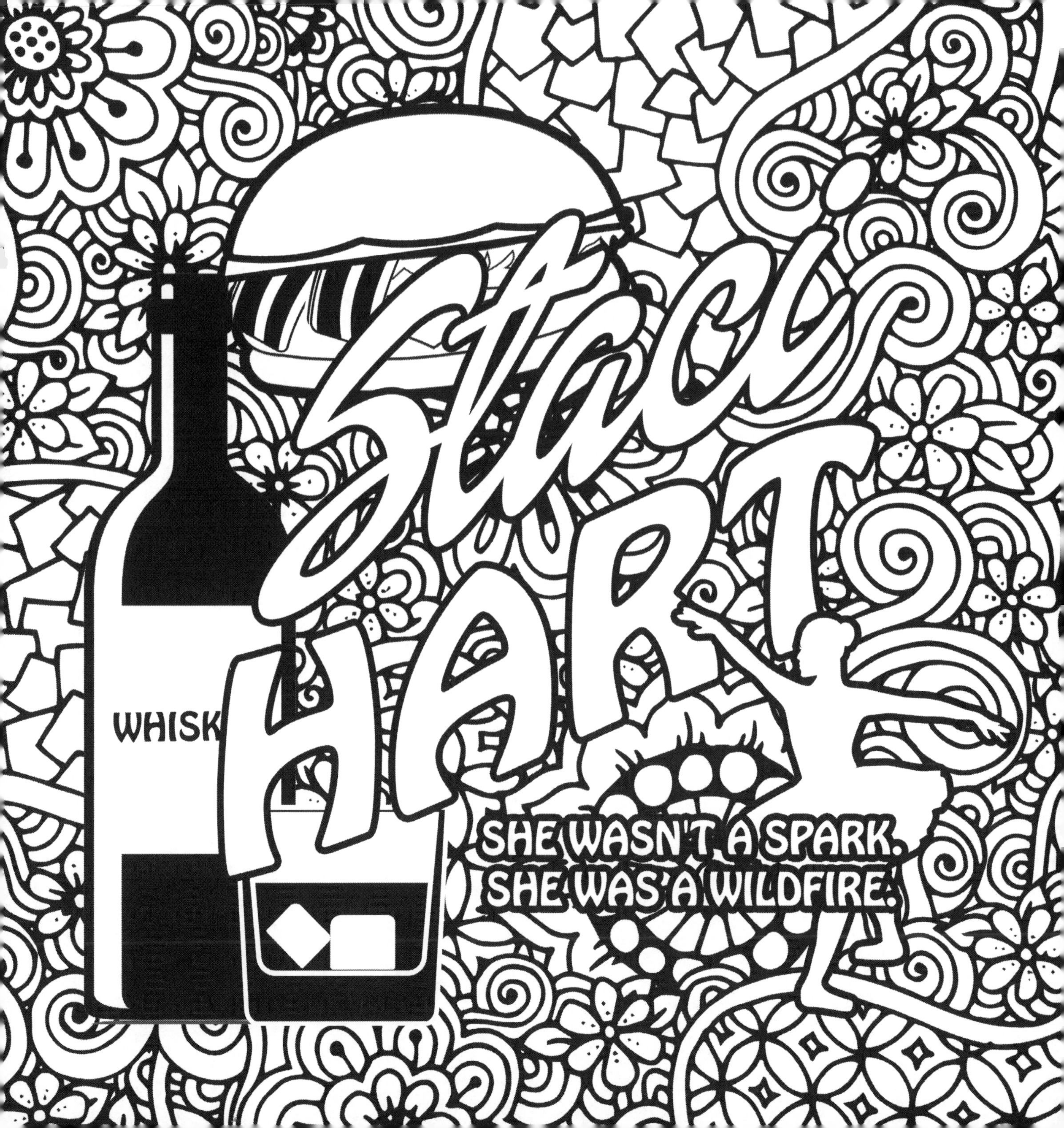
Staci
HART
WHISK
SHE WASN'T A SPARK.
SHE WAS A WILDFIRE.

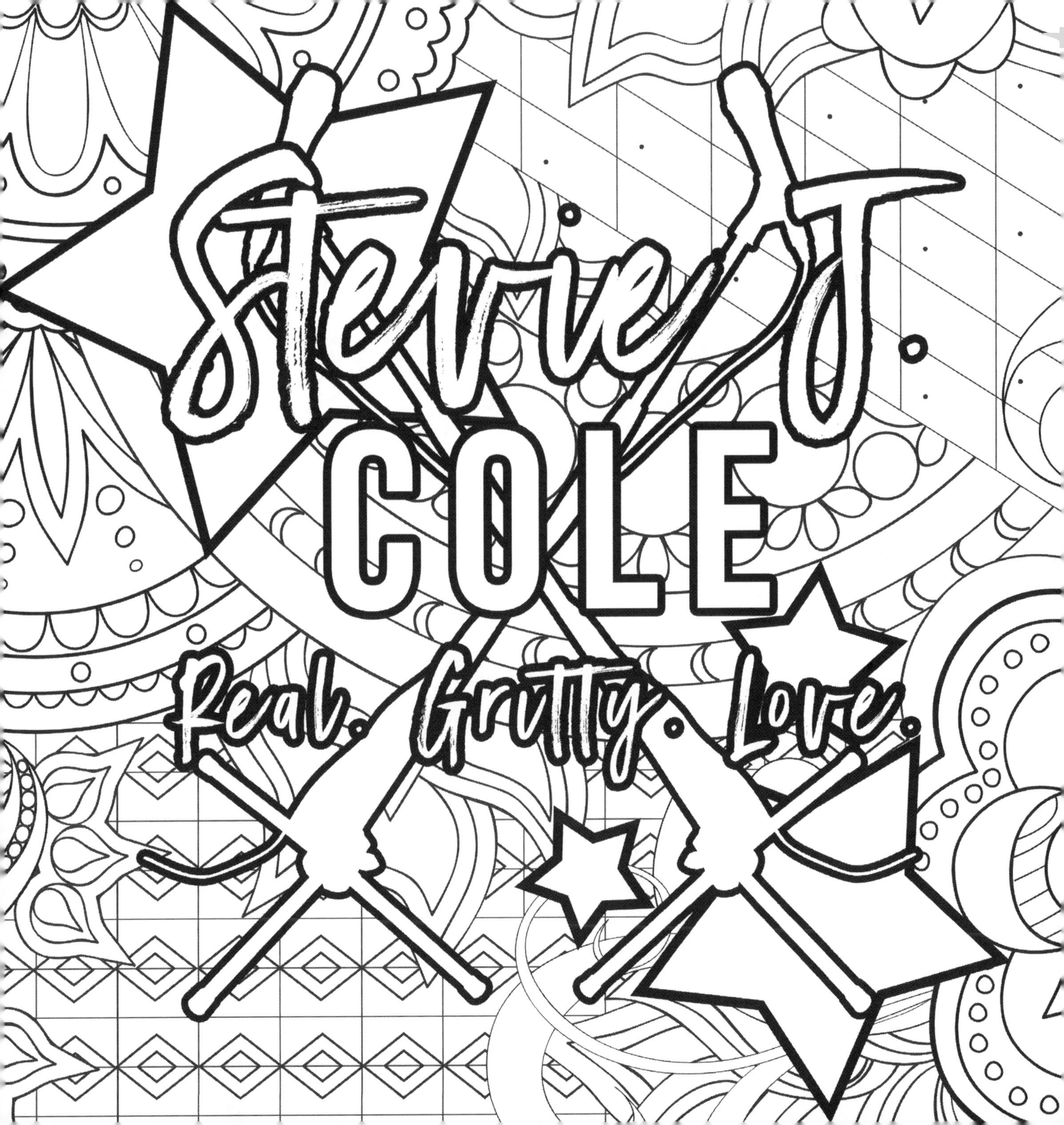
Stevie J.
COLE
Real. Gritty. Love.

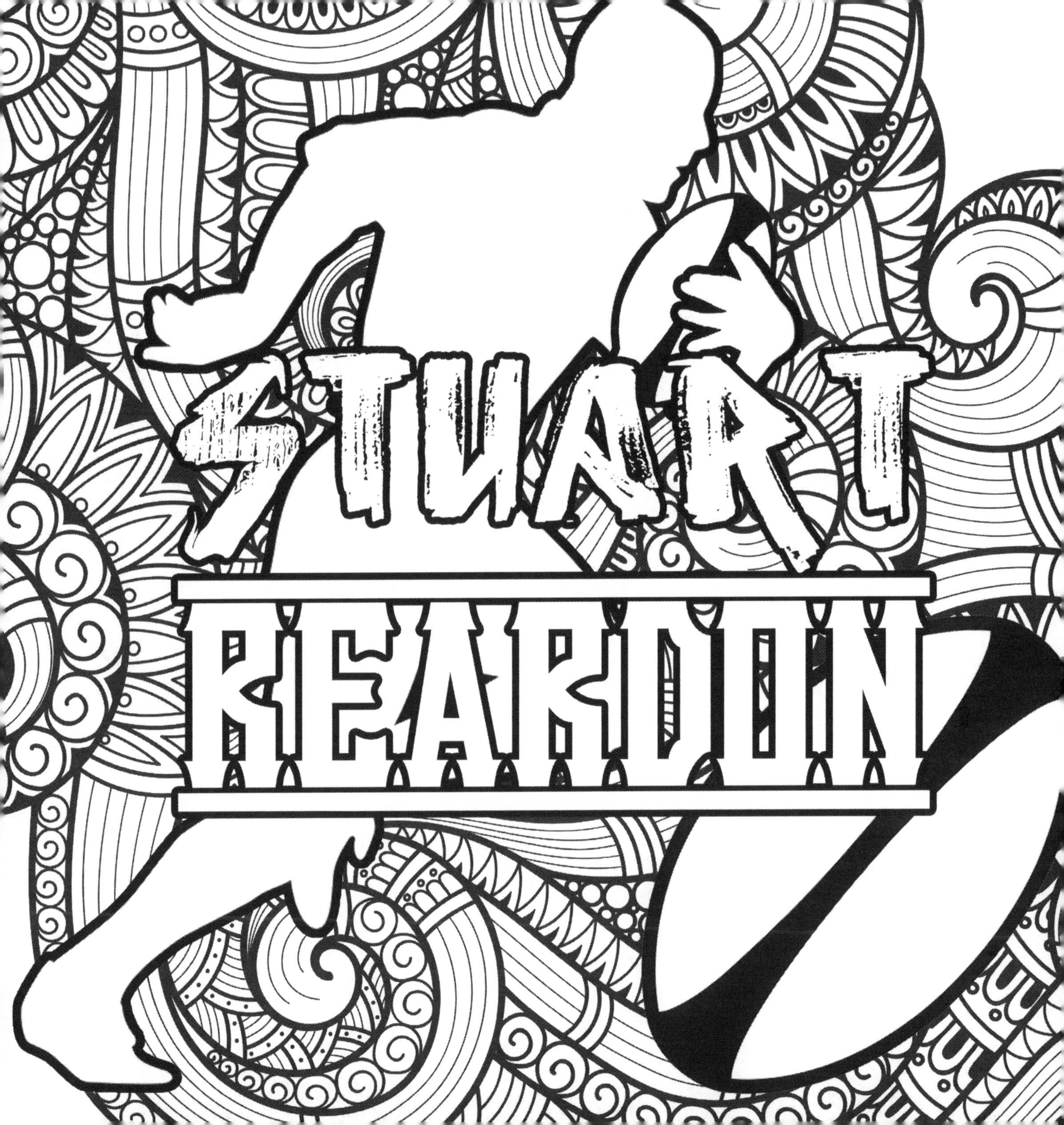
STUART
REARDON

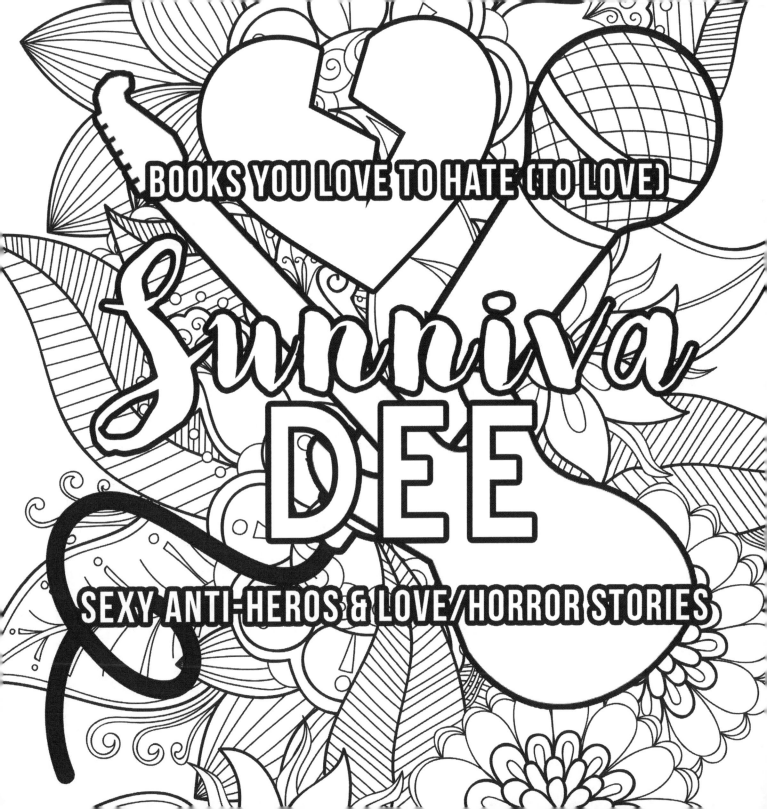

BOOKS YOU LOVE TO HATE (TO LOVE)

Sunniva
DEE

SEXY ANTI-HEROS & LOVE/HORROR STORIES

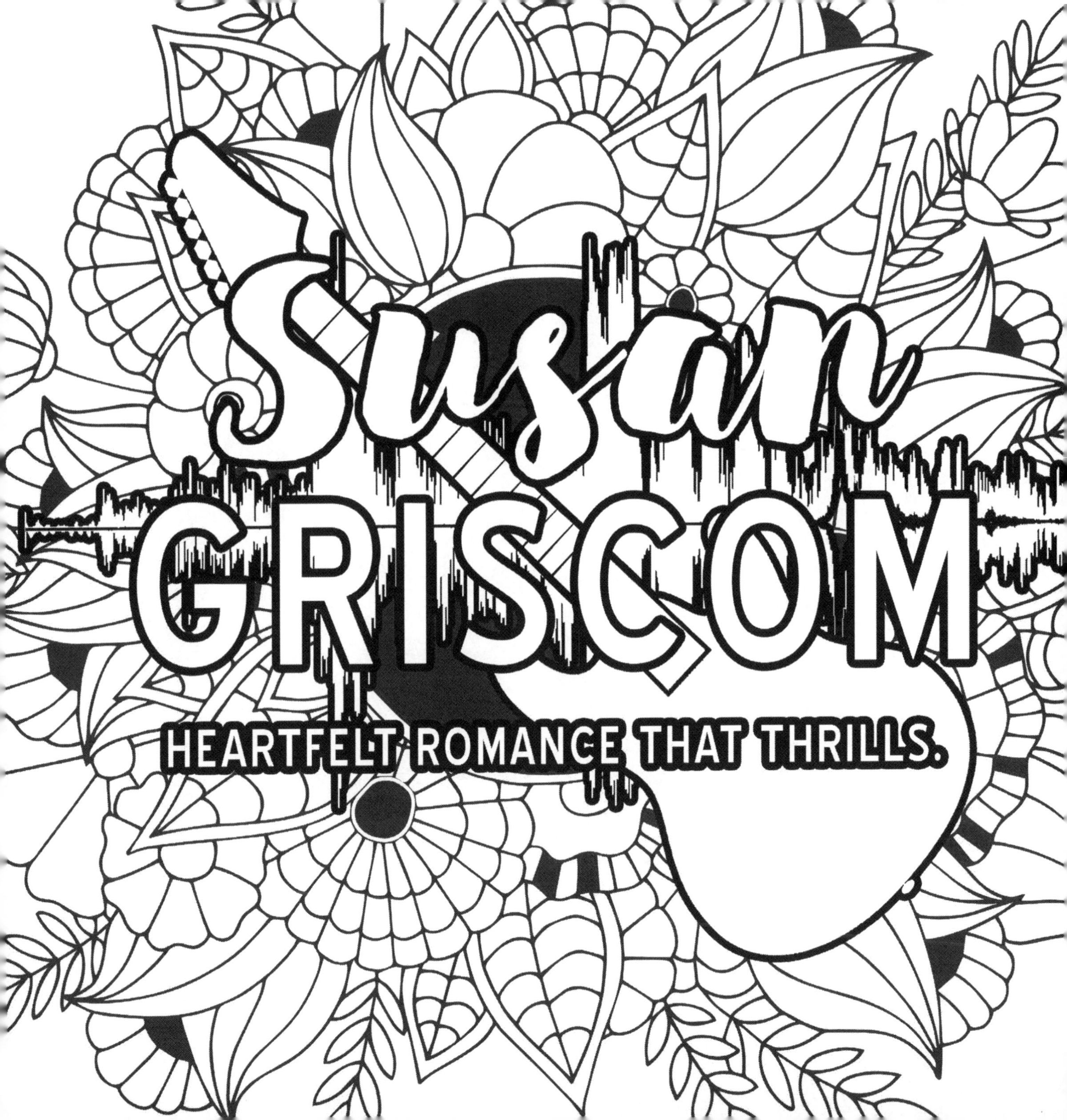
Susan
GRISCOM
HEARTFELT ROMANCE THAT THRILLS.

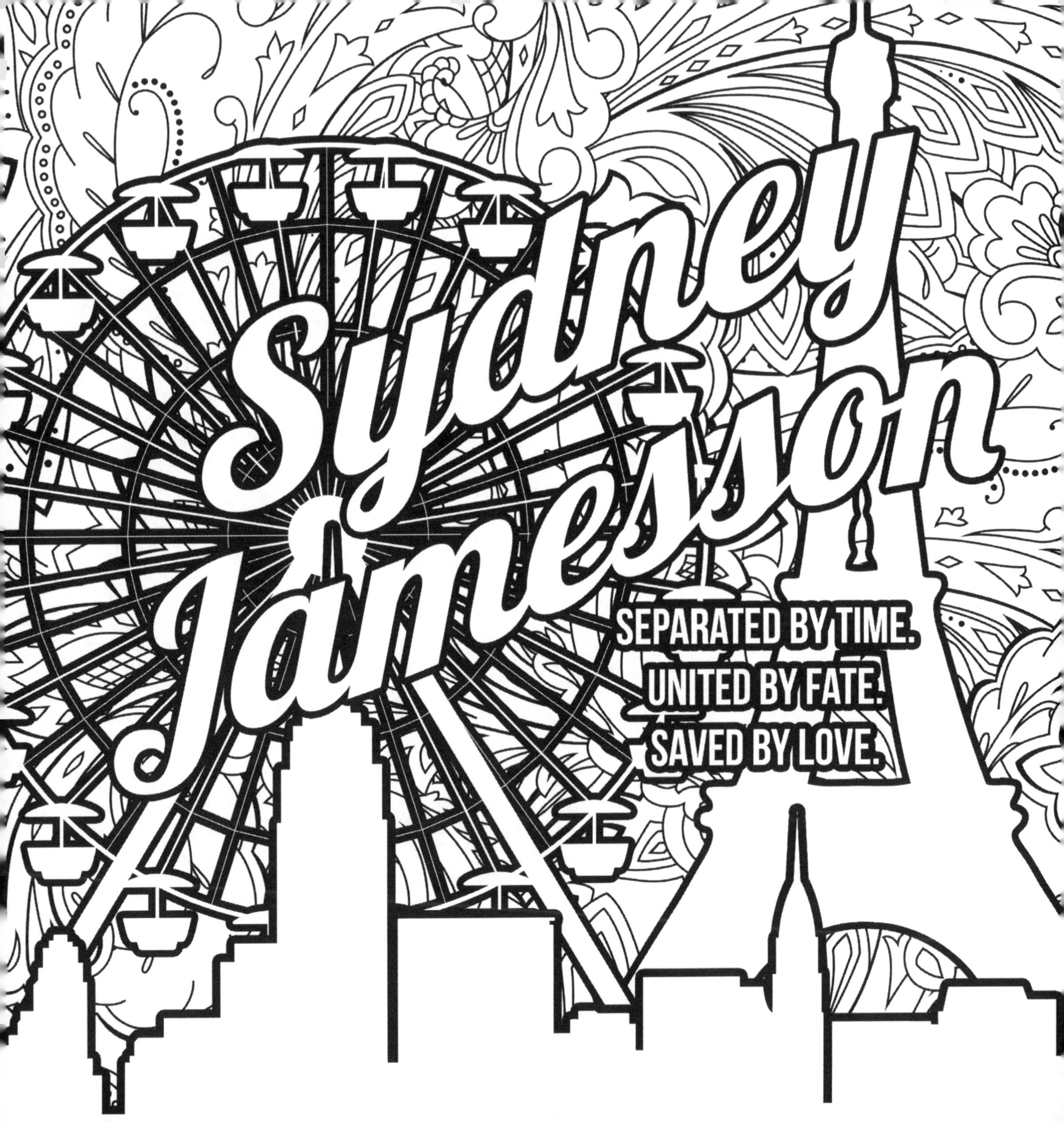
Sydney
Jamesson
SEPARATED BY TIME.
UNITED BY FATE.
SAVED BY LOVE.

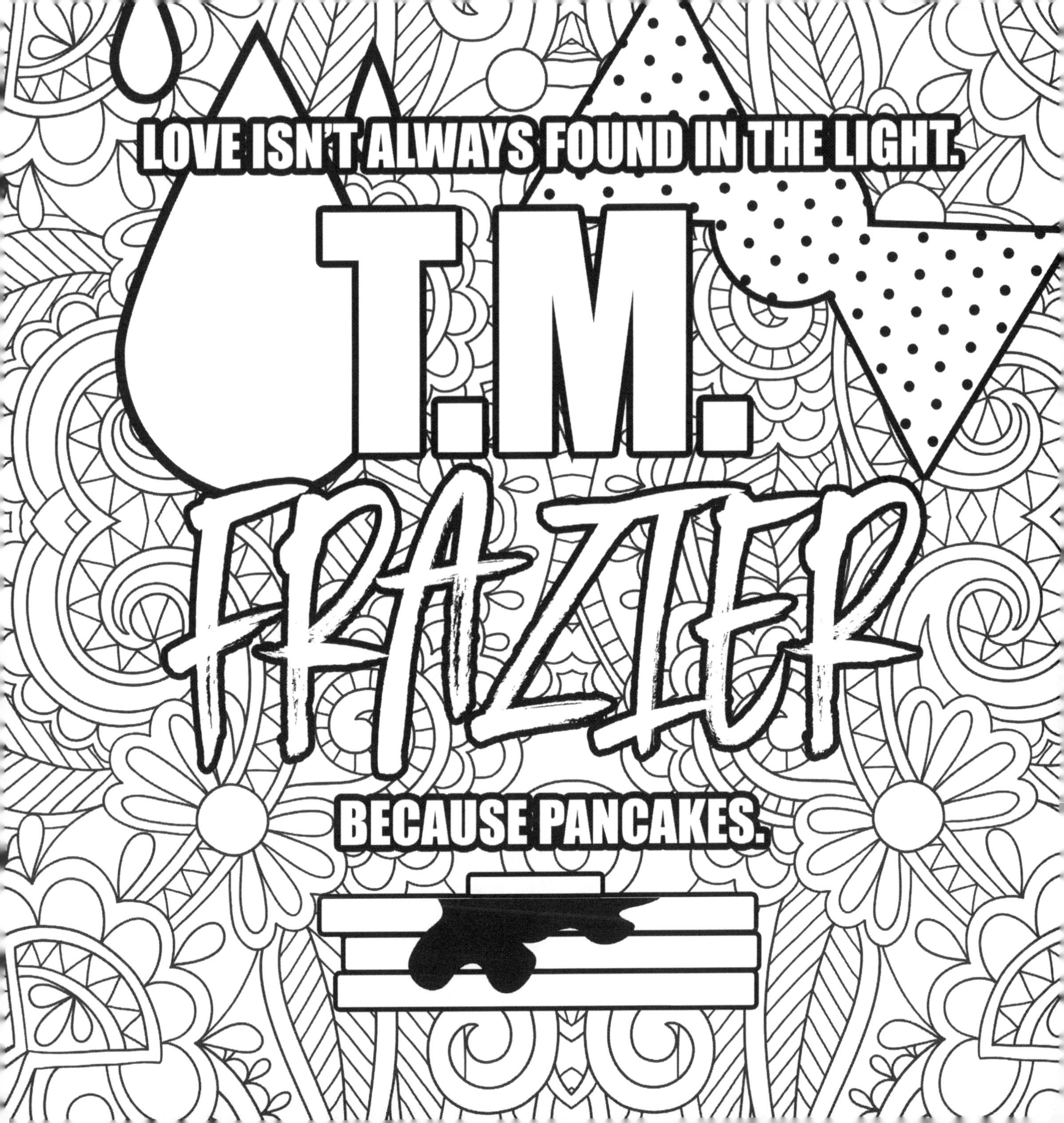
LOVE ISN'T ALWAYS FOUND IN THE LIGHT.
T.M.
FRAZIER
BECAUSE PANCAKES.

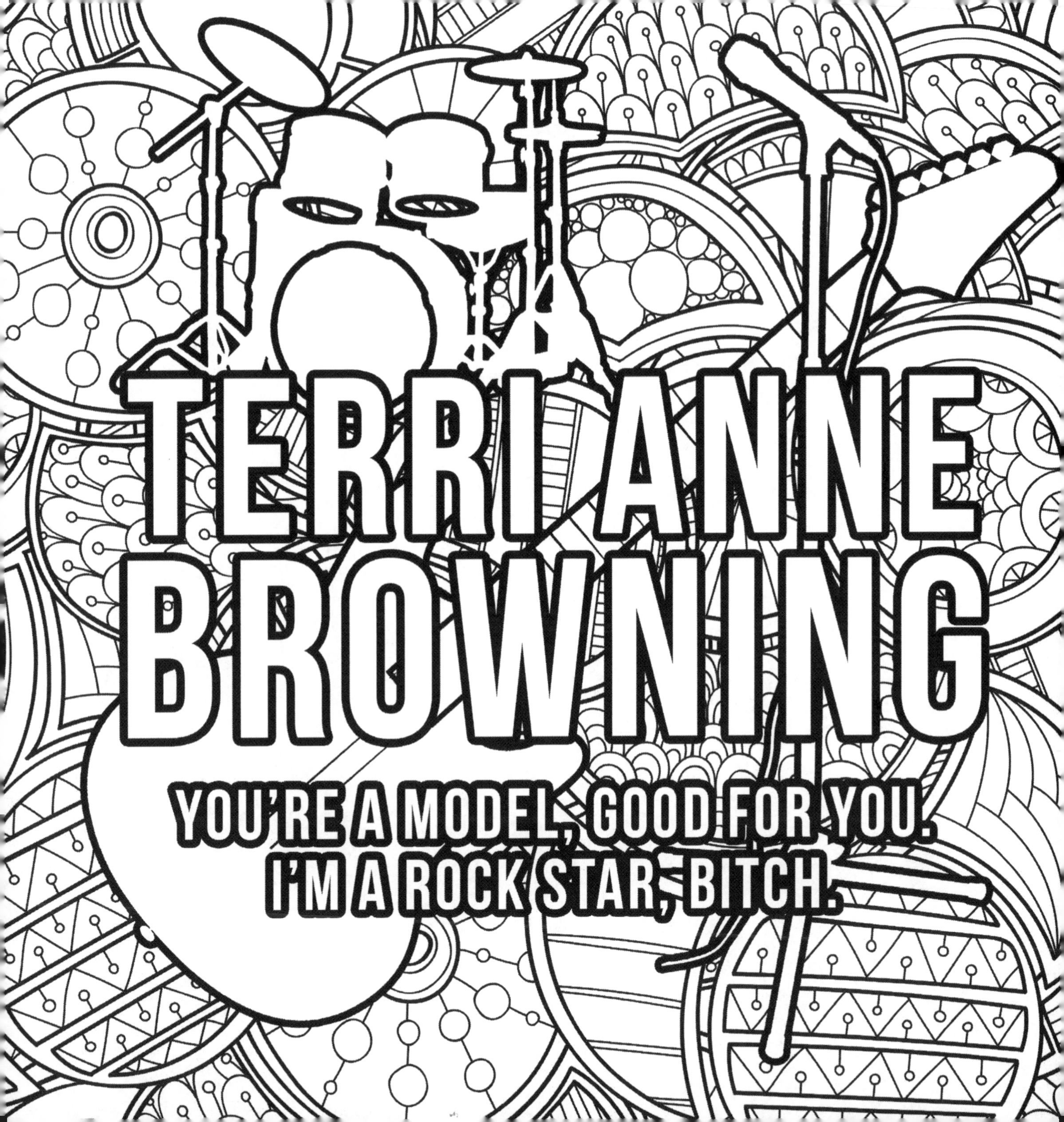
TERRI ANNE
BROWNING
YOU'RE A MODEL, GOOD FOR YOU.
I'M A ROCK STAR, BITCH.

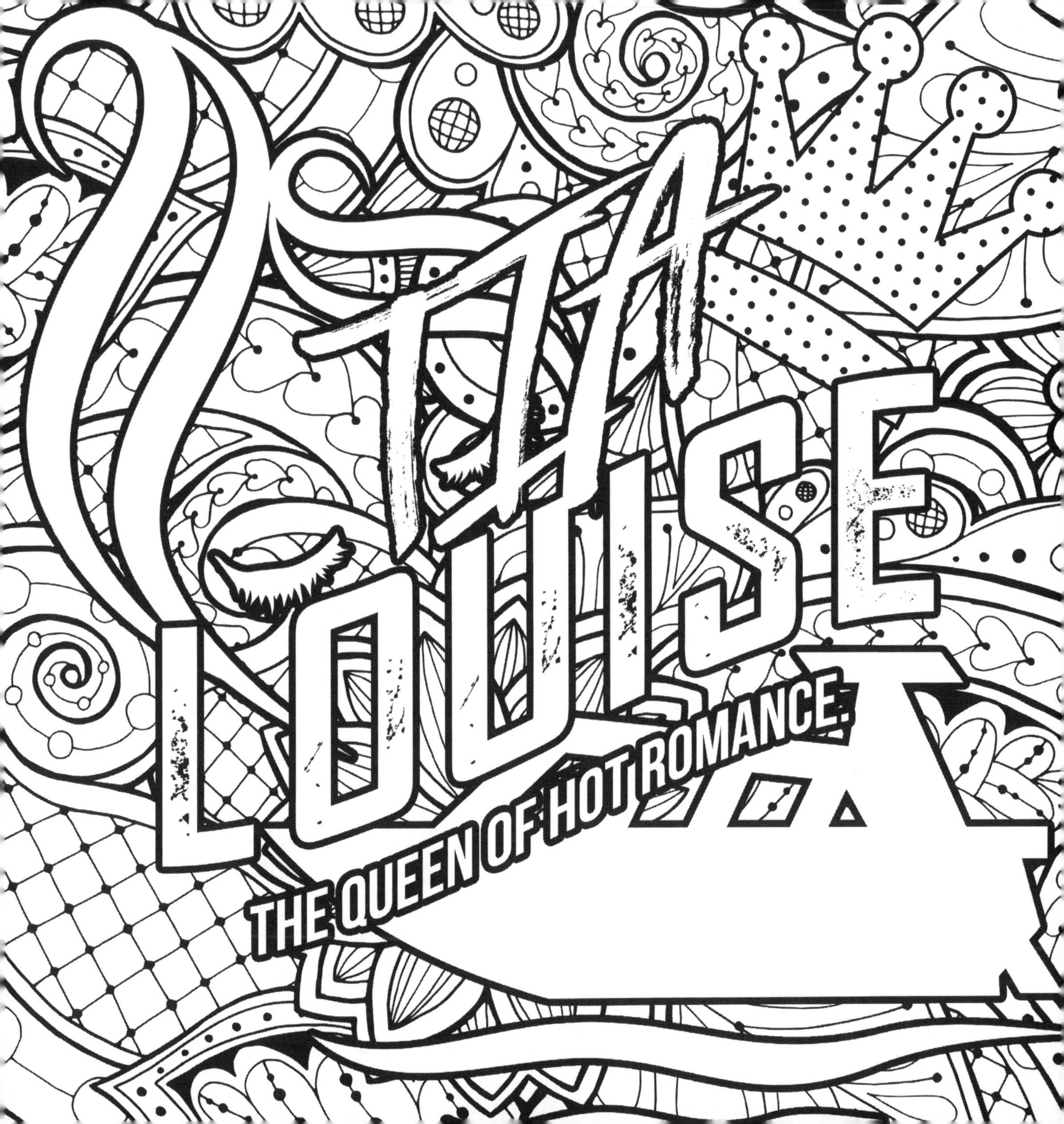

TIA
LOUISE
THE QUEEN OF HOT ROMANCE.

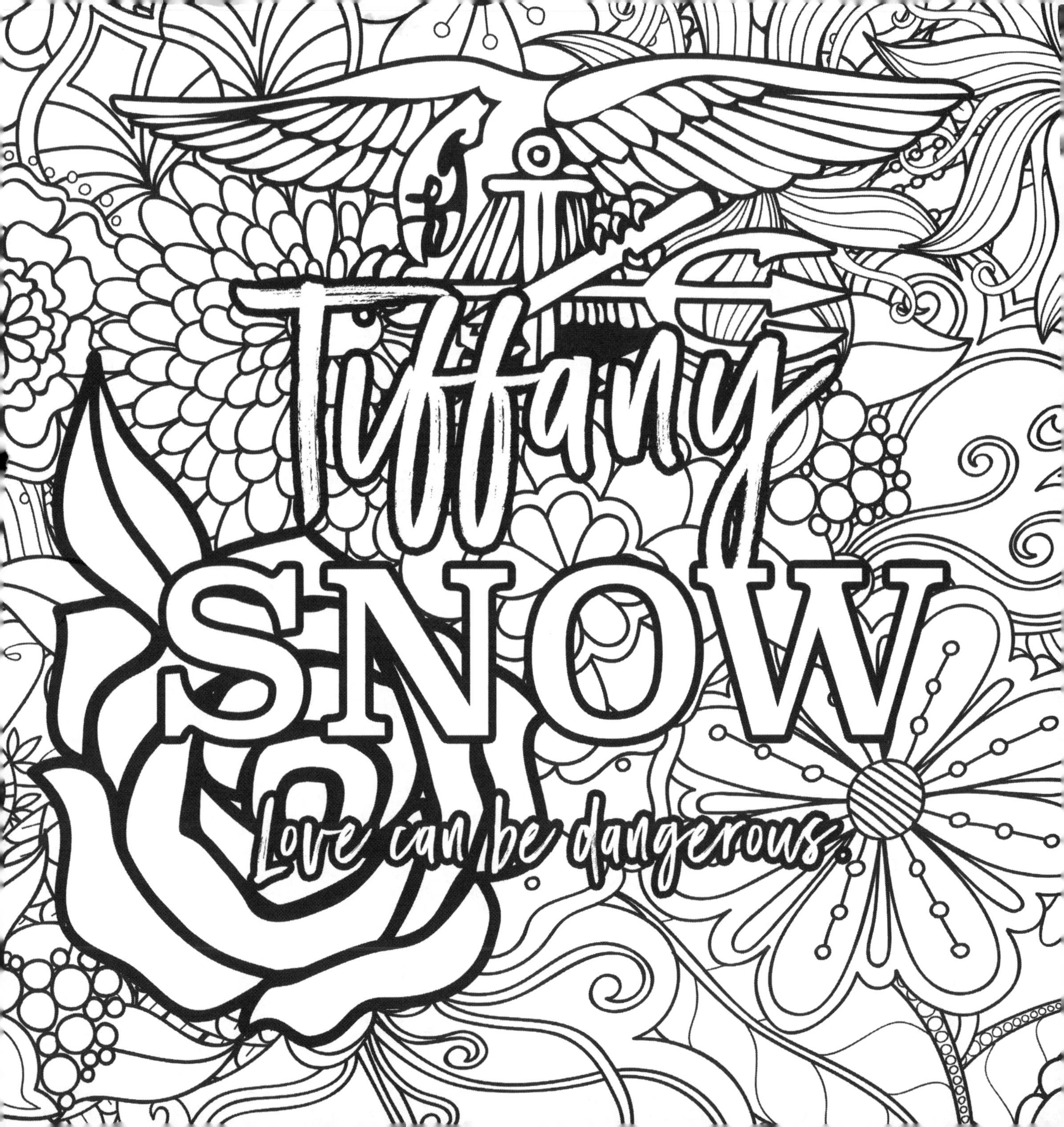
Tiffany
SNOW
Love can be dangerous.

35189916R00084

Made in the USA
San Bernardino, CA
18 June 2016